KV-476-753

Reading Success

A Guide for Teachers and Parents

BRENDA THOMPSON

SIDGWICK & JACKSON
LONDON

First published in Great Britain in 1979
by Sidgwick and Jackson Limited

Copyright © 1979 Brenda Thompson

ISBN 283 98517 8

Printed in Great Britain by
A. Wheaton & Co., Exeter
for Sidgwick and Jackson Limited
1 Tavistock Chambers, Bloomsbury Way,
London WC1A 2SG

READING SUCCESS

By the same author

LEARNING TO READ

LEARNING TO TEACH

THE PRE-SCHOOL BOOK

FIRST FACTS (series editor)

Acknowledgements

The author and publishers are grateful to the following for permission to quote from their copyright material: Constable and Co. Ltd for *Penny Buff* by Janetta Bowie; and Penguin Books Ltd for *Penguins in Schools* by Cliff Moon and Bridie Raban. They would also like to thank the following for permission to reproduce illustrations from their publications: Lund Humphries Publishers Ltd for *The Visible Word* by Herbert Spencer; Initial Teaching Co. for *ita and your child;* George Philip Alexander Ltd for *This is my Colour* by Derek and Lucy Thackray and *Watch Me* by Terry Hall; Heinemann Ltd for *The Great Big Enormous Turnip* and *The Bus Ride;* and Collins Sons & Co. Ltd for *Beginner Book Dictionary* by Dr Seuss and *ABC Word Book* by Richard Scarry.

Contents

1 Introduction

New thinking

Reading is the first and most important skill children learn at school. If they do not learn to read well the rest of their education will be impaired. We are right to worry about both the children who fail to read at all and those who become only poor readers. But I believe too much emphasis can be put on failure. A negative school of thought has grown up too much concerned with all that would possibly go wrong with the many parts of a supposed reading mechanism. I feel we should be far better off studying the reasons for success, and applying these lessons to the children who seem to need extra help.

My philosophy is that you learn to read by reading. From this simple precept a number of things follow: that you learn to read better by reading more; that you learn to read really well by reading plenty of interesting, relevant material of high quality; and that motivation is more important than methodology. For me, success in reading is a function of the time spent on it. It also follows that if you avoid treating reading as a mechanical ability you do not then sit back when a child is 'able to read'. Instead you encourage him to go on practising his skill in order to become an ever more accomplished reader.

Some years ago, in a book called *Learning to Read*, I criticized ways in which children were being hampered in learning to read, chiefly by boring, irrelevant and confusing reading schemes that imposed a mechanical interpretation of reading. Since then the development of an entirely new theory of reading has lent powerful support to my ideas. The study of 'psycholinguistics' has revealed the dominant role of the mind in reading and the way in which it actively searches for meaning. A child's mind is so eager to find meaning that the beginning reader, when faced with texts that do not make sense, will provide his own interpretation. 'Read what is there,' the teacher insists, 'and not what you think is there.' Psycholinguistics encourages an approach to learning to read which stresses motivation, materials and practice that encourage the search for meaning. Psycholinguistics reduces the case for methodology and mechanical 'skills', demonstrating that these might actually restrict meaning.

Skills and shibboleths

Before I go on to talk about some of the fascinating implications of psycholinguistics for learning to read, it is only fair to say that the entire problem of how reading works – profoundly important as it is for the way reading teaching is organized – rarely has a critical bearing on whether or not a child will learn to read. Most ways of teaching reading work, most of the time, for most children. Overall this is a great blessing. It is also a nuisance. For it means that every teacher of reading can be sure the particular method she favours is the right one and can produce the results to prove it. Few people have the temerity to suggest that children learn to read in spite of the patent methods rather than because of them.

A survey of the literature on learning to read shows that its authors for the most part go by appearances. They are unconcerned with the controlling function of the mind and preoccupied with the eyes, the ears and the voice. Reading is carefully explained .as a package of artificial skills whereby visual information (i.e., words on the page) is 'decoded' into sound (i.e., the equivalent of speech) and thence into meaning. Success, it is implied, is the perfect co-ordination of these learned skills. Failure occurs when there is a malfunction of one or other of the organs or the links between them. Often the 'decoding' process is described as quite independent of 'meaning'. The typical textbook on the teaching of reading is therefore full of phrases such as 'visual discrimination', 'auditory discrimination', 'word attack', 'left–right orientation', 'hand–eye co-ordination' which seem to emphasize the purely sensory nature of reading. These concepts are described but never explained, as they are held to be self-evident. It is perhaps time they were rigorously re-examined.

This is not the task I have set myself. I do not intend this book to be a full-scale critique of typical books on the teaching of reading, even if such a study of the conventional wisdom is overdue. I do feel it would be enlightening if I suggested the flavour of such books and their background assumptions. I shall do this by looking closely at a typical shibboleth of the textbooks: left-right eye movements. For this one notion illustrates the faults of the mechanistic explanation of reading, in being pseudo-scientific, in patronizing both children and teacher and denying their intuition and ingenuity, in divorcing 'reading skills' from reading itself, and in putting the blame for failure squarely on those who fail.

Pupils

Everyone would agree that in English the ability to read a line of print from left to right is an essential accomplishment. But does that mean that the eyes need special training? John M. Hughes in his book *Reading and Reading Failures* warns that 'it is extremely important that primary skills are well-developed before a child starts reading, in order that the habits of regular, rhythmic, horizontal eye movements can be established... the child who is pushed into reading before he has these controls may develop tensions and faulty eye habits.'

It is one thing to give a helpful reminder of a convention of written English. It is quite another to erect this convention into a dogmatic and oversimplified visual explanation of reading that suggests the eyes need a sort of visual ping-pong programme before they are ready for reading. Mr Hughes is not alone in assuming that the eyes of the beginning reader are somehow untutored and weakly muscled. His and others' simplistic explanation ignores all that has been known for a long time by scientists about the remarkable efficiency of human vision, even in a five-year-old. The eyes when reading do not work like windscreen wipers. In a child, as in an adult, the eyes make many purposeful movements that are rapid and intricate. Some of them are imperceptible. None of them can be taught. In fact, it is a hundred years since Emile Javal discovered that 'the belief still widely held... that we read as our eyes sweep smoothly along the printed line, is false. In reality our eyes move along a line of print in a series of small rapid jerks, but because these movements are so fast no clear vision is possible and perception occurs only during the fixation pauses which punctuate these jerks.' My quotation is from *The Visible Word* by Herbert Spencer, who goes on to mention the eyes' 'backward movement, called a regression, towards the beginning of the line. Regressive pauses help to correct inadequate perception.' Poor readers make more regressions and beginning readers have constantly to go backwards.

As reading is a form of seeing, there seems very little point in trying to alter the eyes' normal way of working, as directed by the brain, and forcing them into unfamiliar and limited movements as directed by the school master. Left–right eye training is at best a complete waste of time and at worst a hindrance. Yet the doctrine persists, and some teachers seem prepared to go to extraordinary lengths to train their pupils' eyeballs. A letter appeared in *The Times Educational Supplement* recently from a school 'where we have been using eye exercises for five years with remedial readers'. It went on to claim that 'failure to co-ordinate the eyes for fine movements is an indication of deficit at the cortical development stage which should take place at about the age of eighteen months, and that it springs from earlier failure at the pons and mid-brain levels of development at about six months and one year respectively.' This language is more reminiscent of a brain surgeon than of a teacher. In fact, as Frank Smith says, in *Understanding Reading*, trying to control eye movements in reading may be like trying to steer a horse by its tail.

Distinctive features

Frank Smith is an English professor working in Canada and one of the most powerful and stylish advocates of the psycholinguistic theory of reading. He has written several stimulating books about reading, *Understanding Reading, Psycholinguistics and Reading* and *Reading*, which are light years ahead of most books on the subject. His books contain many complex arguments and references which it would be wrong to attempt to summarize. I shall try to hint at some of the arguments and examples. An impressive amount of research into the nature of vision and mind supports the psycholinguistic viewpoint and disposes of the idea of reading as a sort of clockwork mechanism to which the teacher alone holds the key.

Let us examine a typical clockwork assertion. Messrs Daniels and Diack in their book *The Standard Reading Tests* mention that 'visual discrimination and orientation is not something which like Topsy – just grows. Children have to *learn to see*' (their italics). But children bring to the task of learning to read already developed mental and visual powers, without which reading would be an inconceivably difficult task. They already know how to see. What they have to learn is where to look, and what to look for, in order to make sense of written language. The only way to learn the visual rules of language is by doing as much reading and writing as one is able. Does anyone think for a moment that an adult who decides to learn Chinese has to learn to see first? Yet equally, no one would dispute that he would make little progress without learning to distinguish the features of each Chinese written character. His learning would be helped by the capacity of human vision to appreciate general features of written words or symbols. For example, we can come across the same word in different typefaces or in different handwriting where its shape can vary enormously, yet we can always recognize it because of certain features that are always present. We may find them next to impossible to analyze and certainly we cannot teach them. Psycholinguists call them 'distinctive features'.

The human knack of spotting 'distinctive features' explains why the chemist can make sense of the doctor's scrawled prescription when the computer cannot read *Janet and John*. What the computer *can* do is be programmed to read a specially designed script. In technical jargon what the computer does is 'template matching' and what the human eye does is called 'feature analysis'. The difference is more than a matter of mere jargon: feature analysis involves some astonishing arithmetic.

People whose mathematics have become a little rusty may be surprised to learn that the old party game 'Twenty Questions' can theoretically cope with over a million objects. For each question represents two choices: 'Yes' or 'no'. And two to the power of twenty – that is, two multiplied by itself twenty times, amounts to 1,048,576. The point of this example is that a 'twenty questions' approach to language would be quick and efficient. The eye and the brain between them would make a series of quick decisions about features of language and on the 'twenty questions' analogy would be able to deal with a huge number of alternatives. However, Frank Smith estimates that just five distinctive features are theoretically sufficient to distinguish *all* the letters of the alphabet.

If reading does make use of feature analysis, there is no need for children to be taught to read as if they were computers scanning programmed symbols. However, it does sometimes require a little time and practice to be sure of the 'distinctive features' of letters and words. This is how five-year-old Abi Apampa wrote his name the first few times, **Aloɪ Ajooɪmjooɪ** until he realized that the distinctive features of certain letters depended not just on a combination of shapes but on the way these shapes were joined together.

The speed of vision

We next look at some laboratory evidence about vision which involves the tachistoscope. This is a device which gives a split-second exposure of an image, for example, a word or picture. It allows scientists to measure how quickly, and how much, people see and remember. Tachistoscope experiments have produced some surprising results. The first surprise is that, whereas the eye can take in an image in an astonishingly brief moment, as little as fifty thousandths of a second, it takes the brain five times longer to deal with it. At first sight it looks as if the eye is a brisker, more efficient instrument which has to wait for the poor old brain to catch up. This is not so. The eye's greater speed is simply an expression of the brain's dominant role in vision. As the servants of the brain, the eyes provide at each instant more information than the brain could possibly use. The brain selects from an otherwise overwhelming mass of information the items that make sense. For example, reading is the business of making sense of otherwise senseless marks and spaces on the page.

Reading is therefore as much a mental process as a visual one. We might find it easier to accept the mental nature of reading if we did not attach so much importance to the eyes. We say 'I see' about things we understand and are certain of. We say 'I think' and 'I hear' when we are less sure. The eyes are the windows of the soul but there is no such status for our ears, less lovely, less expressive organs. Is that because we learn spoken language in advance of written language? It does not occur to us that our ears do not actually hear separate letters and words but a stream of complex vibrations of the air. The brain has to make sense of it all. So we happily accept in spoken language that we do not normally memorize the words we hear. We hear for meaning. We get the gist of what is said.

The hardest part of reading

The second surprise of tachistoscope findings is that whole words can be identified as easily and as quickly as individual letters. This happens even when none of the letters in the words are 'discriminable', having been deliberately half-covered or otherwise obscured. In one brief exposure the brain is capable of taking in four or five unrelated letters of the alphabet. But it turns out it is equally capable of taking in three or four unrelated words, pushing the letter score up to nineteen or so. If the words were in the form of a sentence, the score would rise to thirty or so letters. This finding seems to be literally one in the eye for the letter–by–letter school of learning to read. Why bother to learn letters if you can learn words, and why bother to learn words if you can learn sentences?

There would of course be a ready rejoinder which we should have to take seriously: that beginning readers are quite different from established readers. I recollect a tart comment to this effect in a recent book about reading. 'Reading has been described as a so-called psycholinguistic process. This is what happens with mature readers. It has nothing to do with beginning to read.' It is true that the chief technical difficulty of teaching and learning reading is getting started. You cannot get children to re–cognize, i.e., to 'know again', letters, words and meanings they did not know in the first place. However, what this argument overlooks is that, although beginning readers have a huge problem, they do not come to it totally unequipped. They bring to the reading task three sets of equipment they have already acquired: highly developed visual and mental skills, linguistic experience, and the human mind's appetite for meaning.

Discovering the rules of language

We marvel at the way children grow and learn in their first few years but we sometimes fail to give them credit for their remarkable intellectual achievements. A child who begins reading is commonly thought of as starting at zero. Yet he has already mastered the pattern of language, in particular the naming of things. Communication and the need for it are not mysteries. As Frank Smith says, 'Basically a child is equipped with every skill that he needs in order to read and to learn to read: all that he needs is to discover the particular rules that apply.' The first half of this statement is a truism for the great majority of children. The second part describes the reading teacher's proper task, which is to help children discover 'the rules'. They are rules which are so numerous and complex, that no one has ever enumerated them or pinned them down, least of all in a grammar book. They could certainly never be equated with the 'phonic rules' often mentioned in reading textbooks. Besides, these phonic rules are in themselves far more complicated than is popularly supposed. American researchers Berdiansky and Cornell summarized phonic rules into 166 rules and 600 exceptions (see Chapter 2). Such a mass of rules must be seen not as 'steps to reading' but as a deterrent. The only way to approach a learning task as complex as written language is by trial and error. Children can only discover the rules of reading while they are reading. The teacher cannot teach these rules. The child must work them out for himself. It is the teacher's job to provide guidance and 'feedback', as the beginner most of all needs to know if he is right. He is bound to make mistakes but is also bound to learn from them. The more he reads the more he comes across the same words in differing settings and contexts, and learns the rules associated with them.

What we really mean by these rules is: firstly the statistical evidence that everyone stores in his unconscious mind as to the incidence of letter combinations and words in the language, and secondly the shades of meaning he has built up for every word. Although, when reading, a person is not aware of applying precise mathematical probabilities, he nevertheless has an exact notion of which groupings of letters are more likely to occur, which word is likely to come next in a phrase, and which words are common and which rare. As soon as a child learns his first word, which is usually his name, he is beginning to absorb the rules of written English. For, however imaginative the name, it must conform to certain likelihoods. Let us take the name **Tracy.** T can be followed by a vowel or by one of three consonants 'h' 'r' or 'w'. Tr can only be followed by a vowel and so on. The sound of the 'a' is made long and the 'c' soft by the 'y' at the end. The more a child reads the more he will meet these likely combinations, and needless to say will not encounter the letter combinations absent from English. Every time he comes across a word he will unconsciously test and refine the rules. He will link them with the rules he already has, from his spoken language of likely word orders and probabilities. Therefore, providing he does not make so many mistakes that he is discouraged, a child will learn best by reading more.

Guesswork

If the child is given plenty of reading material at the right level of difficulty, he will be able to predict unknown words from the context. A child expects written language to have as much meaning as spoken language. He applies the same criteria for reading as for listening: a plausible sequence of events, a likely sounding remark, a happening or gesture borne out by the illustrations in his reading book. If he meets a new word he guesses, then looks for the teacher's encouragement. Has he got it right or not? Unfortunately the beginner's logical and potentially fruitful strategy may be thwarted. Although beginning reading material may be strong on recognizable characters, what they are actually *up to* is often extremely vague. There is seldom a story line that carries the meaning. It hardly needs repeating that the language of beginning books is often stilted and unnatural to the point of nonsense. But it is also worth emphasizing that this makes the text totally unpredictable just when it should be *absolutely* predictable. The pictures accompanying early reading texts can be ambiguous or even irrelevant.

Yet the biggest obstacle to trial and error strategy is the teaching attitude that makes guessing both academically and morally wrong. Most reading tests penalize guessing. Teachers who feel they have to pounce on mistakes will put paid to the good guesses along with the bad. In a way there are not good and bad guesses. For if you guess you are bound to make mistakes. The more guesses you make, the greater your risk of mistakes. The teacher will best help the child if she gives him the chance to correct his own mistakes.* A child who is reading for meaning will go back and reread a phrase or sentence as soon as he realizes that he has not made sense.

I feel the most valuable advice I can give to teachers to help the beginning reader is for them thoroughly to introduce the material the child is expected to read. This is not from the spirit of making things easy for the child. It is partly in order to provide motivation. As we shall see later in the book, young children only want to read familiar story books. They get greatest pleasure from old favourites. The second consideration is a technical one. The fluent adult reader does not take in the letters or words as he reads them, he goes straight to the meaning of the piece. In fact it is not possible to think about letters *and* words *and* meaning all at the same time. The beginner, however, must look at words in order to familiarize himself with them, to learn their rules that we discussed earlier. It helps him to concentrate on this task if he already knows the meaning of the piece he is reading. Furthermore, knowing the meaning makes him better able to predict completely unfamiliar words.

I read a story to a class of six-year-olds and introduced the name of their teacher in the story. They were mystified as to how their teacher got into a story book, so I suggested that they should read it for themselves to see if I had been kidding or not. Several of the children were so overcome with curiosity that they did read the story. The book ought to have been too hard for them since it was not a 'graded reader'. However, familiarity with the context helped them with the difficult words. Reading books to children and getting them interested in the stories is one of the most worthwhile things teachers can do.

---

*I have throughout this book used the convention of referring to the teacher as 'she' and the pupil as 'he', for ease of identification. The majority of primary teachers are women.

Dexterity

We have had a brief glimpse of some of the theoretical aspects of learning to read which I hope, at least, have acted as appetizers. I can only implore those who are concerned with teaching reading to read Frank Smith's books (details in the Bibliography). In my brief look at reading theory I took as an example of conventional thinking the supposed importance of left–right eye movements. I have always felt that this was a typical wrong emphasis. The eyes that follow the left to right sequence of written English also travel from right to left and, in doing so, it turns out that they are running ahead in order to help the brain gather meaning. The fluent reader anticipates what he is going to 'read' by looking ahead at large chunks of the text. It is only in this way that trained 'speed readers' can read several thousand words a minute.

At the simple level of reading common English words, Frank Smith has drawn up an elegant illustration of the way 'right to left' eye movements are just as important, if not more important, than left to right eye movements. None of the following words can be read without looking ahead to the last letters of each word: hot, hoist, hoot, hook, hour, honest, house, hope, honey, where the 'ho' is modified in each case by the ending. There are at least nine different ways in which the pronunciation of 'ho' is changed by succeeding letters. But this is not a trick example. With most English words, to get both the sound and the meaning right, they must be scanned from right to left. So much for a mechanistic and simplistic explanation of learning to read that does not take into account the workings of the mind.

2 Teaching Methods

Sight and sound

Although there appear to be a great variety of methods and techniques for teaching reading, in the end they boil down to two. One is 'phonics', the other is 'look and say'. All the rest are modifications or refinements of either the phonic method, which places greater emphasis on the sound of words, or the 'look and say' method, which sets greater store by the appearance of words.

In spite of extravagant claims on behalf of newly marketed techniques, and heated arguments between supporters of rival methods, most teachers play safe by using a mixture of methods. The Bullock Report, *A Language for Life,* surveyed fourteen hundred classes of six-year-olds and found that both phonics and look and say were used in ninety-seven per cent of them. So it hardly seems that they are regarded as alternatives. What counts in practice is the stress put upon one or the other method. Let us look first of all at some aspects of phonics.

Sound patterns

The pro-phonics teacher would explain how the sounds of letters relate to the sounds of words. She would start by teaching the children the sound that each letter makes. She would go on to combine letters into two- and three-letter words and later into larger and more complex words.

Simple and self-evident as this sequence seems to many teachers, we know from what we have already learned in studying the theory of reading that there are many pitfalls.

We know that it is probably a mistake to believe that the beginning reader decodes from letters to sound and then from sounds to meaning. However, leaving such conceptual matters aside, there are technical difficulties in building words from sounds. Paradoxically, the children who ought to benefit from an 'elementary' approach, i.e., the youngest children and the slowest learners, are most affected by such difficulties. In my observation many children between four and seven years old can become fluent readers well before they are able to break down and synthesize groups of sounds.

The first stumbling block in phonics is the impossibility of pronouncing consonants without an accompanying vowel. If we try to sound out the letters of the word c a t for example, we cannot avoid saying something like 'ker' 'a' 'ter'. However hard you try, you cannot get rid of the extra 'er' sound. The technical term for this sound is a 'schwa'. It was described as 'a ball and chain for the young reader' by Gertrude Baldwin in her interesting book *Patterns of Sound*. Miss Baldwin has devoted a lifetime to making phonics fun, and to trying to run consonants and vowels together more smoothly. She has done this by a combination of mouthing exercises, which draw attention to the position of the lips, tongue and teeth in sound, and by a series of alliterative rhymes and games. Unfortunately her claim that an initial consonant is a 'get ready letter' that has no sound until it is given 'a sound maker', i.e. a vowel, while an ingenious way of getting round the 'schwa' problem, is misleading. Miss Baldwin's technique does not solve the main problem for the small child of carrying a sequence of sounds in his head while he works out the way they might modify each other, whereupon he might recognize the meaning.

Complications

We see once more that 'pure' phonics imposes a triple task:

first, the recognition and sounding of individual letters, then the appropriate blending, and finally the elucidation of meaning. The Baldwin technique also reflects a general preoccupation with initial consonants. The 'getting ready' idea is often expressed more aggressively by educationists in the phrase 'word attack'. Frank Smith has demonstrated how much more prudent it is, rather than attacking a word head on, to look at the end of the word first. Suppose you were building a certain word by the classic phonic method: say this word began with the letters w a . Even with a number of simple words you would find yourself back-tracking almost immediately. There would be a totally different phonic outcome according to whether the sequence ran w a s, w a s h, w a s t e, w a r, w a r y, etc.

Another way of getting past the 'schwa' hurdle is to group letters so that 'c a t' becomes 'ca t' or alternatively 'c at'. Although this improvement helps to remove one problem it does not make phonics any easier – for instance, it increases the number of basic sounds to be learned. For while there are only twenty-six letters in the English language there are forty-six sounds, or 'phonemes' as they are called. It follows then that most letters have more than one sound. Children have to learn each letter and the sounds they make. But that is not the end of the matter. The same sound can be made by different letters and combinations of letters. (The classic example of this is George Bernard Shaw's pronunciation of 'ghoti'; 'gh' as in enough, 'o' as in women, and 'ti' as in station.) This increases the number of phonic building blocks to the point where phonics can no longer claim to be simple but has to be seen as rather complex. Attaching vowels to initial or final consonants pushes the number of the possible combinations to be learned into the hundreds.

Seventy-nine rules for six vowels

Vowels present the greatest difficulty. They have the

greatest number of variations in their sounds. They are often silent, for example in the final 'e' which teachers often refer to as the magic 'e' because it modifies previous vowels, e.g. 'ic*e*', 'mad*e*' and 'hom*e*'; and where a vowel is 'lost' in a vowel combination as in 'me*a*t', 'ra*i*n', 'he*a*d'.

The letter 'a' has quite different sounds in simple words such as 'cat', 'cake', 'call', 'was' and again in words with double vowels such as 'steak', 'breadth', 'weak', 'rain', 'said'. It can be seen that vowel letters and sounds do not correspond in English in a simple and easily learned way. Furthermore, vowels are the sounds most affected by regional accents. For example, 'u' and 'a' sounds are often so close in London speech that London children find the difference hard to cope with. My experience with adult illiterates has confirmed the perverse and slippery nature of vowels. Just as you have got 'breakfast' established, along comes 'steak'. I have found that by using a combination of 'phonics' and 'look and say' I have been able to bring adult illiterates to a reading age of eight or nine, but they have still been unable to synthesize regular three-letter words from their individual sounds, largely because of the stumbling block of vowels. It may still be argued by the proponents of phonics that all the various sound combinations fall into well-defined groups plus, they admit, a few exceptions which can be taught as a set of rules, still making phonics the most logical and manageable approach. Any teacher will see it as worth the effort to teach the child a set of rules that will make him independent and able to read alone, but seldom is the size and nature of this effort calculated. American researchers Berdiansky, Cronell and Koehler (in a technical paper quoted in *Understanding Reading* by Frank Smith) worked out the extent of the 'phonic rules'. They started with 9,000 different words forming the typical vocabulary of six to nine year olds and then analyzed the 6,092 one- and two-syllable words. They finished up with 166 phonic rules and no less than 661 exceptions. Not surprisingly, a large number of rules – seventy-nine in all – are needed to deal with the six vowels.

Conventionally, reading teachers demonstrate the vowels in strict sequence, starting with the short version, for example 'a' as in 'cat', 'e' as in 'bed', 'i' as in 'hit', 'o' as in 'hot', etc. However, from the very start of language, vowels are just as likely to occur with all their sounds. 'Was' is as likely to 'has', 'to' is as likely as 'hot'. The only way of avoiding the problem is to stick to boring phonic drills or rigidly contrived and usually nonsensical texts.

Considering how long it would take to teach 166 phonic rules, not to mention the 661 exceptions, I find it hard to believe that teachers ever actually complete the task. In my experience children pick up many of these rules in the course of their reading before the teacher formally teaches them. Although phonics seems to offer precise information, in reality all it can do is to suggest clues to pronunciation. A child must effectively know a word before he can read it, in order to know which of the phonic rules apply. As Frank Smith points out, 'Even if a reader did happen to know the seventy-nine rules that are required to account for the pronunciation of the six vowels he would still have no sure way of telling which rule applied or even that he was not dealing with an exception.'

The cat in the vat

To make matters even worse for the beginning reader and the teacher, the words we most commonly use are the ones that have diverged most from their logical spelling. It seems that the more a word is used the more its pronunciation alters. The American researchers mentioned earlier gave about ten per cent of words as exceptions but of course that does not take into account the number of times they are used. I have looked at lists of words in common use by children, first of all the well-known key words that form the basis of the Ladybird reading scheme, and secondly the slightly different list of *Words Your Children Use* (compiled by R.P.A. Edwards and Vivian Gibbon for the Leicester Education Committee). In both cases one third of the words are exceptions. This accords with Sir James Pitman's estimate when developing his case for the initial teaching alphabet that one third of words are phonically regular, a third are irregular and a third obey no known rule.

To teach reading by a rigidly phonic programme demands the avoidance of many commonly used words, and the emphasis on regular three- and four-letter words leads to some rather odd texts. My favourite is the following surrealistic extract from a Victorian School Board Reader:

> He is a bad lad. Did the mad lad rub the cat? No but he led the ox to the wet hut. She is to wed Pat. He hid the cat in the vat. The fat Kid got in the mud. Ned fed the ox. He got a cod but he did not get a kid or a cat.

Such a text now strikes us as extremely quaint because most modern phonic programmes admit the need for a number of irregular but highly useful words to be learned by the 'look and say' method. These words, generally referred to as 'sight words', make the text of early readers more assimilable.

The Cat in the Hat

The famous 'Beginner Books' of Dr Seuss deliberately exploit the zany aspects of phonic alliterations. These books do not represent a structured, controlled vocabulary reading scheme but teachers find them useful to help children learn and practise phonics. The titles of some of these books, *Hop on Pop, The Cat in the Hat, Fox in Socks,* give an idea of the approach. They are to be seen as phonic-flavoured nonsense, whose brilliant style and outrageously comic illustrations are irresistible to children (and very difficult to imitate).

Whatever method of teaching reading is used, at some point the child will need to learn phonics. We all need to know the variety of letter/sound correspondences, and this is something that children can begin to learn almost as soon as they start school. As we have seen the amount of knowledge needed to build words phonically is enormous and this task is better left until children have grasped the principles of reading and the nature of written language. It is only through experience of reading that children realize that words occur in families, that certain combinations of letters and words are more likely than others, and that phonics can be used as an analytical tool.

I know beyond doubt that phonics works as a method of teaching but anyone who uses it as the main approach should be aware of the risks involved. It can penalize the youngest and slowest children who lack the intellectual equipment to synthesize words. It can spoil the enjoyment of reading through an over-emphasis on mechanics at the expense of meaning. Even for bright children it is an unnecessarily slow process.

In my earliest days as a teacher I was required to teach reading by the phonic method and having learnt to read that way myself, assumed that it was logical. However, I was made to ponder when I realized the children were learning to read faster than I could get round to teaching them their phonic rules. I was surprised to find that children were happily reading words that they were as yet incapable of building. From what I now know of how language works, I realize the children were learning to read by sight and were making considerable use of contextual clues.

A large contribution to the success of phonics is the tendency for the child automatically to learn by sight the words he is sounding. In children's writing there is sometimes a revealing mixture of visually familiar words and phonically derived ones. The other day a little girl wrote that there were 'buglos for hedicad people' (bungalows for handicapped people) in her street and her favourite TV programme was 'lef aleipics' (Laff Alympics). The phonic words reveal their meaning when spoken in an adenoidal cockney accent.

Which words should be taught first?

'Look and say' is self explanatory. The learner reader looks at a word. He is told what it says. Then he himself says it. After a number of repetitions he remembers what the word says without being prompted.

Usually the teacher begins by showing the children a limited number of 'flash cards'. A flash card is a large card with a word printed on it in lower-case script. In spite of their name flash cards are held up long enough for the children to have a good look at them. The cards are re-introduced in various ways as many times as necessary for the children to learn them. However quickly the children learn, to begin with they can cope with only a few words. Which words then should be taught first? Normally the teacher will use the flash cards associated with the first words of the reading scheme she is going to use. The beginning vocabulary of the scheme can only be arbitrary. The obvious criteria are those of simplicity and familiarity. It is worth stressing that there is no special significance to most of these early vocabularies.

However, the authors of the 'Ladybird' reading scheme have attempted a rational selection of the most commonly used words, which they have labelled 'key words'. Unfortunately this common sense attempt compounds the fault inherent in all 'look and say' primers. Any book based on repetition of a severely limited vocabulary is bound to result in stilted and unnatural language. When the words repeated are solely humdrum utility ones the text is more than usually insipid.

The main criticism of 'look and say' rests on the need for each word to be learned separately. Thus the acquisition of a working vocabulary is thought to put too big a strain on the beginner's memory. The child appears to lack any means of coping with an unknown word. We have seen that phonics claims to provide a child with a set of tools for breaking up and rebuilding unknown words (but appears to overlook the memory load represented by the 166 phonic rules and 661 exceptions among the 6,000 words most commonly used by children). Strange as it seems, the child who is taught by 'look and say' is not dependent on the teacher for each new word he meets. After he has acquired an initial starting vocabulary that enables him to read simple books, there are a number of stratagems he can employ to work things out for himself.

Built-in clues

The most important clues come from the context of carefully graded and controlled reading material. Most of the words would be known, involving simply recognition. Unknown words involve what Frank Smith calls 'the reduction of uncertainty'. Children expect what they read to make sense. Even for the very beginning reader, syntax narrows the possibilities dramatically. No child substitutes a wrong part of speech, a noun for a verb, a pronoun for an adjective. Nonsense is apparent from the start. To illustrate this I will take the simple sentence 'I like the toys', which I asked a beginning reader to read to me. He read the word 'I' then took a wild stab at 'like' as 'can'. He then stopped short as he was evidently unhappy at reading 'I can the'. I pointed to the word 'the' which he read and he also surmised the word 'toys' from the picture. He then tried the word 'play' and saw that it didn't fit. He then correctly read 'like'. The word 'like' was not inevitable but highly probable. It is a word often used by children (being the fifty-third in order of popularity according to Edwards and Gibbon's *Words Your Children Use*). It is also heavily stressed in early reading material, a convention that my beginner was already aware of. The important point is that he did not have to work through hundreds of possible words. There are a limited number of probable relationships between 'I' and 'the toys' and he did not even have to read it correctly to get the meaning. However, once he had the meaning and checked the word, the repetition of the word 'like' on every page of this reading book ensured that it would be absorbed into his vocabulary. This is a very simple but significant illustration of the various ingredients a reader can use to fill in the missing pieces of his informational jig-saw: they comprise various familiar items, other items that can be guessed from picture clues, plus a general meaning (i.e., based on possible relationships between 'I' and 'the toys' which can be narrowed down by trial and error). Altogether they lead to the acquisition of a new key word which will make the rest of his reading that much easier. Of course, it can be argued that if he had used phonics he would not have made the ridiculous substitution of 'can' for 'like'. However in order to read the word 'like' correctly he would have to be familiar with an advanced phonic rule, the so-called magic 'e'.

Let us now look at a slightly more advanced story and apply similar logic. The following is a passage from *The Remarkable Rat* (a folk tale retold by Mollie Clark):

Rat did not like getting wet so whenever it began to rain

he dug a deep hole and hid in the hole until the rain stopped.

The text is accompanied by a picture of the rat in a hole with raindrops falling above him. There is so much meaning on the page that it would be very easy to omit a word here and there and still make sense. The systematic use of this technique of restoring missing words is called the 'cloze procedure.' When in a passage every tenth word or so is deliberately left blank, the reader usually has no difficulty whatsoever in completing it. All the meanings in this passage support and correct each other so that you could still understand it if you left out all the verbs.

| You do not | getting wet so you | a |
| hole and then you | in it until the rain | |

This shows the necessity for even the earliest reading texts to be so structured as to allow children to predict unknown words with reasonable accuracy. Fortunately children do not have to learn this skill of prediction. They have already acquired it in their spoken language and they bring it ready developed to the reading task. However, I do not need to labour the point that many primers fail to provide a guiding structure, preoccupied as they are with the mechanical repetition of words and sounds at the expense of normal patterns of language and their built-in clues.

Shades of meaning

Any statement in ordinary English not only gives clues to an unknown word but gives each word a specific meaning that a word in isolation cannot have. It is this quality of convergence, of narrowing down upon a particular meaning, that makes learning to read relatively easy, once you have got started. The obvious but subtle analogy is with solving a crossword puzzle. Once you have got a few letters you get along swimmingly – unless you run up against the boundaries of your own knowledge.

I am aware also that there are other forms of language that diverge rather than converge as 'ordinary' language does. Wit, humour, irony, jokes and nonsense can all involve an unexpected twist of language. Poetry, too, is unpredictable compared with our normal 'throwaway' language which is why, I suppose, teachers feel that it has to be learned by heart. There is also the matter of intonation which almost disappears in written language but can sometimes carry the whole of the meaning.

Should we conclude that children can only safely learn to read plain English? It is true that young children are literal-minded and this characteristic probably helps them to 'take things in' faster. Yet some forms of 'unpredictable' language can be used early on in the teaching of reading, for example, nonsense poetry and archaic folk tales. Although in vocabulary terms it is harder to know what comes next, there are other strong pointers such as rhymes and rhythms, favourite phrases and repetitions, and other guiding conventions.

It follows from the idea of words co-operating with each other to produce meanings that many of the most popular words in the English language will have acquired the greatest variety of meanings and shades of meaning. It was noted in the Bullock Report that the most common five hundred words in English have been estimated to share between them over fourteen thousand meanings. Thus the technique of 'look and say' would appear to owe as much to context as to the nature of individual words. Once a core vocabulary of sight words has been learned (not usually more than thirty words), few teachers would attempt to teach words in isolation. If there are too many unknown words in any piece it cannot be read effectively by any method because, quite simply, the reader who reads too slowly overloads his sensory store and short term memory. The visual image lasts for only half a second and the short term memory holds only four or five items of meaning.

F.J. Schonell on word shapes

Ironically, the most used reading test (Schonell's Graded Word Reading Test) depends on children reading unknown words in isolation. F.J. Schonell, the designer of this test and of the 'Happy Venture' reading scheme, was one of those advocates of 'look and say' who laid great stress on the appearance of words. He described four factors which contribute to 'accurate reading or recognition' (sic).

   a) the visual pattern of the words
   b) the saying and hearing of the words
   c) the meaning of the words
   d) the impressions gained through tracing or writing (or trying to write) the words.

Schonell describes in his book *The Psychology and Teaching of Reading* how a four and a half year old boy has begun 'the game of reading': 'Of these four contributors towards recognition' he finds 'the most important is the *visual pattern* of the word'. Perhaps Schonell did not make it sufficiently clear that the general outline of words is only one aspect of their 'shape', thus leading some teachers into over-simplification. The internal shape of a word is probably more important than the pattern of the ascenders and descenders stressed by followers of Schonell. However, as Schonell pointed out, a lot of phonic material presents unnecessary difficulties by using words that look alike – so that some pupils might read 'pig' as 'big' and 'bog' as 'boy'

the visible word

the visible word

From *The Visible Word* by Herbert Spencer, published by Lund Humphries

or 'big' in the sentence 'the pig with a wig did a jig in the bog'.

Herbert Spencer on word visibility

In normal written language an astonishing amount of blurring can be introduced before words become illegible, as long as the more important features are retained. The whole question of legibility has been studied by Herbert Spencer in his excellent book, *The Visible Word,* in which he demonstrates the greater importance of internal pattern as a cue to perception. It is also evident that the top halves of words carry more information than the bottom.

Herbert Spencer mentions that as early as 1898 Erdman and Dodge found that 'subjects recognized words printed in a size of type too small for individual letters to be identified and, on the basis of numerous experiments, they concluded that it is the familiar total form of a word – its length and characteristic shape – rather than its constituent parts, that is important in reading.' I am not of course recommending that children learn to read with other than the clearest texts. Because the beginner lacks the vast store of prior knowledge of the fluent reader, he needs all the visual help he can get.

Although we do not know for sure what the significant factors are in recognizing a word, we can easily see that, with the help of contextual clues, we can reduce the amount of a word visible and even remove it altogether.

Language structures and probabilities

Perhaps the cloze procedure described earlier is the nearest we can come to showing how children learn to read by 'look and say'. When words are systematically omitted from a text the general meaning is scarcely altered because of the interwoven meanings. Even a short statement can stand to

for offset litho printing

for offset litho printing

From *The Visible Word* by Herbert Spencer, published by Lund Humphries

lose a word without materially altering its meaning: 'The cowboy jumped on his   .'

We are almost bound to assume that he jumped on his horse. If the word turns out to be 'steed', 'mount' or 'four-legged friend' that is only a nicety of style. If the missing word is say, 'motor bike' or 'bed,' this will quickly become clear from the context. We now see that children bring to the task of reading their general knowledge, their intelligence, and their already developed understanding of language structures and probabilities.

Using the right kind of texts with normal syntax, providing there are not too many unknown words, 'look and say' can be seen to be a solidly based method of teaching reading which exploits the naturally occurring structures of language. There may be guesswork but it is informed guesswork rather than the fruitless hit-or-miss business its detractors allege.

Variations on phonics   (i) i.t.a.

The most significant and widespread variation on the phonic method is the 'initial teaching alphabet' known as i.t.a. It was designed by Sir James Pitman in 1959. The Bullock Committee found in 1973 that i.t.a. was being used by nine per cent of schools. Pitman's aim was to redesign the alphabet in order to reduce some of the irregularities between spoken and written English. He and his supporters are at pains to point out that i.t.a. is not a *method* but a *medium* for teaching reading, applicable equally to phonics and look and say. Quite clearly however it is a good deal closer to phonic thinking in that it lays great stress on the decoding of letters into sounds and sounds into meaning. From a 'look and say' viewpoint there is no advantage to altering the look of words.

There are forty-four characters in i.t.a. script as opposed to twenty-six in the normal alphabet, which is referred to

how much is experience of how

abcde...xyz...fghijklm...c...uv...

an alphabet designed as part of an experiment to
determine how each of the lower case alphabet could
be simplified by rules which eliminate certain features
affecting legibility

Towards a new alphabet, from *The Visible Word* by Herbert Spencer, published by Lund Humphries

as 'traditional orthography' or 't.o.', by the adherents of the initial teaching alphabet. Upper- and lower-case symbols are the same shape, differing only by size. The upper halves of letters are kept as near as possible to the shape of traditional orthography, the significant changes being to the lower halves. i.t.a. does not claim to represent a complete correspondence of letters and sounds: for example, both the letter 'k' and the hard form of 'c' are kept. There is no attempt to cope with the constantly occurring (and proliferating) neutral vowel of English – 'a' in phonetic script – which occurs in 'th*e*', '*a*', '*a*go', 'inf*a*nt', 'comm*o*n', 'ov*e*r', 'aft*e*r', '*a*gain', 'fath*e*r', 'op*e*n' and many other words in our normal unemphatic speech.

If one allows that sixteen of our normal letters change their shape in upper case and that there are two lower-case forms of a (ɑ), and g (ɡ) there is not a great deal of difference in the total number of characters to be learned initially.

Whereas i.t.a. undoubtedly helps children in synthesizing words phonically while they are reading, and lessens the spelling problem for children learning to write, the drawback remains of eventually unlearning i.t.a. and tackling the ordinary alphabet. i.t.a. supporters make light of this and stress the results of various surveys that seem to show i.t.a. as a superior medium to t.o. for learning to read and write.

The Hawthorne effect

During the 1960s, research studies involving i.t.a. came thick and fast. Seventeen such surveys were assessed in 1969 by Warburton and Southgate in their book *i.t.a.: an independent evaluation* and shown to have varying degrees of subjectivity and skill in experimental design. One important consideration in the apparent early success of i.t.a. was the so-called 'Hawthorne effect'. This is the

The Initial Teaching Alphabet

a apple	a arm	æ angel	au author	b bed	c cat	ch chair	d doll	ee eel
e egg	f finger	g girl	h hat	i ink	ie tie	j jam	k kitten	l lion
m man	n nest	ŋ king	œ toe	o on	o book	ω food	ou out	oi oil
p pig	r red	ʀ bird	s soap	ʃh ship	ȝ treasure	t tree	th three	th mother
ue due	u up	v van	w window	wh wheel	y yellow	z zoo	s is	

From *i.t.a. and your child*, published by Initial Teaching Co.

tendency of people to respond to the novelty of an experimental product or procedure. One can imagine teachers trying out i.t.a. being very keen to master it and to demonstrate their efficiency to those who had vested their trust in them. It is telling that, between two major i.t.a. experiments in London in 1961 and 1966, the differences between the experimental and control groups shrank, leading Warburton and Southgate to the conclusion that 'to take a plunge...the results suggest that the Hawthorne effect has little influence on t.o. classes, but that it appears to account for pretty well half of the considerable superiority shown by the i.t.a. group.'

Nevertheless, for i.t.a. supporters half a loaf is considerably better than no bread and Warburton and Southgate's approval of i.t.a., in spite of heavy qualifications, has been much propagandized. I find it surprising that these experts, who quite rightly adopted a rigorous approach to other people's work, should tolerate severe technical defects in their own survey on the grounds that it was a 'preliminary evaluation'. They blame 'the time factor' for the absence of 'sampling techniques for the selection of local education authorities or schools to be visited and of people to be interviewed', and the lack of cash for the use of only one interviewer, which is very far from approved market research practice.

Running faster

In my opinion two of Warburton and Southgate's conclusions put a time bomb under i.t.a. The research evidence, they decided, as opposed to the 'verbal evidence', suggested that i.t.a. was more effective for bright than for dull children. Teachers know that bright children are almost bound to learn to read; what they are looking for is a way of making things easier for the slow learner, and they might have expected more of an advantage from simplified spelling. The most damaging conclusion of the independent evaluation was that 'after about three years of schooling, the reading attainments of most children taught initially by t.o. are approximately equal to those of children whose initial medium of instruction was i.t.a.' I would deduce from this that i.t.a. may simply alter the order in which reading skills are acquired. It is uncomfortably reminiscent of those modern traffic schemes to move the motorist scientifically around one way streets and in the end gets him from A to B no quicker than a horse and cart in 1901.

One of the main supplementary claims made for i.t.a. is that it encourages writing by diminishing spelling difficulties (whether by extension it encourages creativity is an open question). However, one of the practical reasons for getting children to write is to give them spelling practice which, by definition, i.t.a. cannot foster. Another observable disadvantage of i.t.a. is the way the i.t.a. child is cut off from other printed messages by which children practise their reading in an incidental fashion: such things as labels, packets, signs, TV captions and so on, not to mention every other book and periodical. For economic reasons only a limited number of books can be produced in i.t.a. script and acquired by a school using it.

Another serious deprivation is of the interest and help of those parents who are bewildered by what seems to them a foreign language. Although the i.t.a. foundation claims that parents are helped to understand, this would be true in my observation only of those parents who are curious about, and eager to help with their children's education. Other parents, especially those harassed by their social conditions, are likely to feel that the mental effort is beyond them. The rather inconclusive benefits of i.t.a. seem to me to have been purchased at a high educational and social cost.

Variations on phonics   (ii) annotation

Other ingenious methods of simplifying phonics involve colour coding and so-called 'diacritical marking'. Both are ways of annotating words in order to indicate different sounds. Colour coding can range from comprehensive methods, such as those of Dr Caleb Gattegno, who tries to give every sound a different colour code, to relatively simple ones such as the 'Colour Story' reading programme devised by J.K. Jones. Children are expected by Gattegno to learn all their sounds, and how to decode and synthesize words, according to a comprehensive and systematic programme on turgidly American lines. The technique is too complex to have found much favour in this country. (Caleb Gattegno, *Reading with Words in Colour.*)

Jones uses only four colours of letters, although some black letters are superimposed on coloured squares, triangles and circles. Again this method is not widely used here. Altogether the various colour schemes are used in six per cent of schools. Criticisms commonly levelled at them are that their elaborate design is too distracting and that materials are limited to those specially published and not available outside school.

Diacritical marks have been in use for centuries as a way of giving extra help to the reader by drawing attention to the different sound values and functions of letters. Bullock found that diacritics were in use in only two per cent of schools. The best known method is one designed by E. Fry ('A diacritical marking system to aid beginning reading instruction', in *Elementary English*) who, with unusual modesty, produced a research survey which did not find his own method to be superior to an unmarked reading scheme.

Variations on 'look and say'   (i) language experience

Both phonic and 'look and say' reading schemes have been

criticized for their restricted language, which fails to reflect the child's own world. The 'language experience' approach purports to allow the child to produce his own reading matter by writing down his own words or dictating them to his teacher. The justification is that children will be more highly motivated to read about their own activities and interests. Children can read back their statements on their own, as a group or as a class. The teacher may develop and extend the work by asking children to copy out words and sentences or to match them to printed cards.

At first sight this would appear to be the ideal method of teaching both reading and writing. It is effective with the latter but as a reading programme it unfortunately lacks structure and progression. Children's own writing is short of the planned repetition which is the *sine qua non* of early reading materials. It does, of course, have a lot of natural repetition of high frequency words, the bulk of children's writing being too limited and repetitive anyway. Less commonly used words can come and go without being learned. Children's handwriting can also suffer from being illegible, with words and lines running together. Context, syntax, grammar and interest are often duller than the worst reading scheme. Nevertheless the act of writing words and reading them back must help a child to learn them. The crucial problem is that it is a slow process and the child's reading ability is likely to run far ahead of his writing ability. Let us compare a page of a child's 'reading and writing book' with a page of a reading book that the same child is capable of reading.

This is me playing out in the garden.

This represents a day's writing by one five year old. Let us look at a page from her reading book (p.36 of book 3a of the 'Ladybird Key Words Reading Scheme'):

Here are some trees and flowers.

Jane and Peter want some flowers.
Some flowers for you and some for me, says Jane.
Get me some flowers, Peter.
Get some for Mummy, and get some for Daddy.

This is a day's reading by the same five-year-old. Her reading capacity is at least five times greater than her writing capacity and includes controlled repetition of useful words.

Variations on 'look and say'   (ii) 'Breakthrough to Literacy'

'Breakthrough to Literacy' is an attempt to use children's own experience as a method of teaching reading while removing their handicaps of their own handwriting. This technique, devised by David McKay, Brian Thompson and Pamela Schaub for the Schools Council, provides ready printed words to be made up into sentences. The word cards can be slotted into a folder called the 'sentence-maker'. This gets round the slowness and illegibility of children's handwriting but not the lack of planned repetition and vocabulary control, and the low output of readable material.

In my experience, a child's own writing is of only cursory interest. Although children are capable of creative writing, not all children are bursting with interesting things to say all of the time. They frequently will oblige the teacher's demands in a quite perfunctory way and their writing will give them little satisfaction in the rereading. On the other hand children will read a favourite book over and over again. Like yesterday's newspapers, children's own 'news' lacks appeal the next day. Often the chore of making up their own sentences persuades some children to keep their news to themselves.

Other criticisms levelled at language experience, and 'Breakthrough to Literacy' in particular, are that it is bitty, and that, as a corollary of the lack of planned repetition, it is difficult to monitor progress.

In spite of my reservations, which amount to stressing once more there is no single magic method of teaching reading, I would recommend 'language experience' as the best method for parents who wish to help their pre-school children to read at home. It is completely flexible and can be tailored to the individual child and his rate of progress.

3 Reading Materials

Evaluating reading schemes

I cannot repeat often enough that what counts for most in the teaching of reading is the skill and enthusiasm of the teacher. A good teacher can make any method work. This does not mean, however, that the materials used are of little consequence. On the contrary, they matter a great deal. A good teacher can be even better with good materials. An inexperienced teacher can be guided and supported by the right kind of materials. Yet there seems to be no general agreement as to what the right choice should be.

British schools are free to decide for themselves how they go about the teaching of reading, and they demonstrate a wide variety of policies. In one school you may find a single reading scheme in use. Another may have several. A third may have no scheme at all but lay stress on something called individualized reading. A fourth may have few books and concentrate on 'programmed reading kits'. A fifth may swear by audio visual aids and use such things as cassette recorders and headphones instead of books. However, most schools will make use of one or more reading schemes supplemented by other books or non-book materials.

So we should begin our evaluation with reading schemes. My intention is not to define the best or the worst reading scheme but to try to discover the criteria which will help us choose the right set of tools for the job. In my view there would be little point in recommending a single reading scheme because none of the existing reading schemes fulfils all children's needs all the time.

Before we develop our selection, let us examine the general justification for reading schemes and any other highly structured reading materials such as 'programmed kits' and 'laboratories' (of which more later). Reading schemes have always come in for criticism, but for most teachers they remain the mainstay of their reading programme. The reading scheme offers a smoothly graduated path for the learner, with plenty of actual reading practice; frequent repetition of familiar words; gradual introduction of new words; continuity of style and content; and helpful format and illustrations. They offer a structure the teacher can rely on. They encourage systematic measurement of the children's progress. Children quickly respond to the progress implicit in the graded readers. Thus there are built-in rewards. Of course, by the same measure, there are built-in discouragements for the slower learners. And unfortunately the drawbacks of reading schemes are all too evident. More often than not their material is thin, artificial, difficult and altogether lacking in nourishment for hungry young readers.

I believe that there are six points to look for when choosing a reading scheme, and the same criteria apply to devising a graded system of non-scheme books. They are:

1 good syntax
2 child appeal
3 a good story
4 good pictures
5 ease of reading
6 a sense of progress.

Good syntax

It should go without saying that a reading scheme ought to

be written in good, clear, familiar and predictable English. Why then is the prose of so many reading schemes strangulated and difficult? The reason is simple. Most schemes are based on the frequent repetition of a limited number of words so as to ensure thorough learning of them. In addition, phonic reading schemes are at pains to use only phonically regular words. Unless a great deal of imagination is applied, the texts produced under these constraints lack the meaning and the rhythm the reader is looking (and listening) for.

> Come here.
> Come and see.
> See the aeroplane.
> Janet look
> Up up up
> See my aeroplane
> Up up up
> Look Janet
> See my aeroplane
> Down.

(*Janet and John,* by M. O'Donnell and R. Munro. Nisbet)

And sad is Nat the big fat cat. Nat tugs Rag Bag in the mud. Mum has Rag Bag. Sad red Rag Bag. And Bad is Nat the big fat cat. Rag Bag fat and red and in bed. And is this Nat, the big bad cat?

(*Language in Action.* Macmillan)

tom must pump it up. pam stops as it is mumps. mum pops up a mess. tom met sam in a mist. tim stamps on a nut.

(*Reading with Words in Colour,* by Caleb Gattegno. Educational Explorers)

Jane and Peter play in the water.
They like to play on the boat.
Come on, says Peter
Come on the boat
Come and play on the boat
Jump up. Jump up here .

(Ladybird Key Words Reading Scheme, by W. Murray.
Ladybird)

The last example carries more meaning than the others but shares their wooden style and sheer lack of concern for language. There is a dearth of the normal clues that allow the beginning reader to bring his existing skill of predicting meaning from the pattern of language. Clumsy writing can only be read in a clumsy fashion. Writing that paid more attention to the rhythms of speech would surely be easier for the beginner to grasp.

Of course, it is not easy to produce worthwhile texts with a limited vocabulary and high frequency of repetition. One solution to the problem is that adopted by caption books. Here a virtue is made of the necessity of repetition. These simple books have the same sentence on every page, except for a change of noun which can be predicted from the illustration. They give the child instant success once he has been told what the sentence is. Hence they are sometimes called 'instant readers'. Here is a good example:

'I am red,' said the tomato.
'I am red,' said the fire-engine.
'I am red,' said the telephone box.
'I am red,' said the cricket ball.
'I am red,' said the pillar box.

"I am red,"

said the fire-engine.

From *This is my Colour* by Derek and Lucy Thackray, published by George Philip Alexander

> 'I am red,' said the poppy.
> 'I am red,' said the mail van.

An extension of this principle are the simple repetitive stories popular with young children. A good example is 'Gay Colour' series published by E.J. Arnold. The Little Yellow Duck asks everyone in turn to get him a fat worm for his dinner but ends up with a piece of string. The Little Blue Jug asks everyone in turn to take him down from the shelf, but gets knocked down and broken by a cat.

The inspiration for such stories lies in traditional tales which often have a repetitive build-up. For example, 'the tale of a turnip' turns up in a number of reading schemes, where everyone joins in a tug of war with an enormous turnip.

Child appeal

I believe that good motivation is the most important factor in learning to read and lack of it is responsible for most reading failures. Children learn to speak because they need to communicate their needs and wants. There is no such urgency about the written word. It is up to adults to provide the incentive and show children that reading and writing are pleasurable as well as useful. If books appear dull to the child, he may not be persuaded of the value of reading: it may seem to belong to annoyingly incomprehensible adult matters. Many early reading books carry the adult stamp. They are worthy but uninspired, as if things associated with school should eschew entertainment. The unfortunate corollary of this is that anything smacking of entertainment could not possibly be educational and allowed in the classroom. Yet children are far more likely to respond to books which are exciting, humorous and attractive.

The mouse pulled the cat.
The cat pulled the dog.
The dog pulled the granddaughter.
The granddaughter pulled the old woman.
The old woman pulled the old man.
The old man pulled the turnip.

From *The Great Big Enormous Turnip* (Scott Foresman Reading System) published by Heinemann

Adults have double standards. They love a gripping novel and may be prepared to stay awake at night to read what happens next. They will not persevere with a book that strikes them as dry and boring unless they have to, for reasons of study. Adults must see equally that children's reading books will be more successful (and children will be eager to learn to read them), if they fall into the first category rather than the second. The more gripping a child finds his book the more he will want to carry on reading on his own. The more plodding his text the more likely he is to read the minimum his teacher requires. Every teacher and parent should take the trouble to observe children choosing books and note what the favourites are. Another test is to see which books in the school library become well thumbed, and worn most quickly. What such books will have in common will be a good story, humour, and lively illustrations. (The school library books I have found needed replacing most often have been those by Richard Scarry and Dr Seuss, and books about dinosaurs.)

A good story

The books children like do not necessarily have to have a plot but there ought to be a sense of what – happens – next. This is where the conventional reading scheme falls down. It is usually built around the minutiae of the daily lives of a sedate, suburban, white, middle-class family. However, the lack of appeal for children has little to do with any failure to identify socially, racially or psycho-sexually. There has been a certain amount of misunderstanding about this and a somewhat unproductive backlash against 'middle-class' reading schemes. Just as 'anyone for tennis' plays were responsible for kitchen sink drama, the reaction to 'Janet and John' produced a stream of books about families from ostentatiously working-class and racially mixed backgrounds. They can be just as boring. For the real reason many children dislike reading schemes is that nothing much happens, and nothing goes wrong. Peter and Jane in the 'Ladybird' series are typical priggish characters. They help Mummy with the tea but never spill the milk. They help Daddy wash the car but never would they turn the hose on him. For them every activity is 'fun' and – would you believe it – 'Yes,' say Peter and Jane, 'We want to go to bed.'

Children do not seek social realism but they do need entertainment. There have been some good attempts recently to get away from the monotony of the perfect family type of reading scheme. Scott Foresman Reading Systems have set out to prove that variety is the spice of reading. Their reading scheme is a mixture of new stories, traditional tales, information and how-to-do-it books, and books of riddles and jokes.

Other series with variety of content and format include Collins's 'Minibooks' and the 'Breakthrough to Literacy' scheme. There are several schemes which show that you do not have to rely on a family for a thematic approach. The 'Griffin' pirate series uses the exploits of pirates and legendary creatures. The 'One Two Three and Away' series uses an ingenious three-cornered village inhabited by families with different coloured hats. The 'Laugh and Learn' scheme is based on the slapstick adventures of a single comic character, Bushy the Squirrel.

Bushy was created by Terry Hall, the well-known ventriloquist and TV companion of Lenny the Lion, who started with an advantage that perhaps few children's reading scheme authors have, an exact knowledge of what amuses and entertains small children. He understands that children feel delicious enjoyment when a character does something naughty or silly that they wouldn't dream of doing, and then gets his come-uppance. In other words, feelings of superiority are more enjoyable than those of identification. The early books of this series demonstrate

build

Builders building a building

bump

burn

I burnt it.

bus

SCHOOL BUS

butter

A butterfly on the butter

button

Big blue buttons

buzz

Bees buzz by.

15

From *Beginner Book Dictionary* by **Dr Seuss, published by Collins**

the art of telling a story with as few words as possible. For example the first book *Watch Me* uses just fourteen words to accompany Bushy's hopping, skipping and flying experiments which land him in hospital. It is a pity that some teachers object to the cartoon conventions of 'Laugh and Learn', and do not get a chance to discover how popular these books can be with children.

Another good example of a simple repetitive story using an extremely small vocabulary is *The Bus Ride* from 'Scott Foresman's Reading Systems'. Each page depicts a different creature getting on a bus. 'A hippopotamus got on the bus,' 'a rhinoceros got on the bus,' etc. In the end a bee gets on the bus and the other creatures are seen hurriedly getting off.

Good pictures

The above examples show just how vital the illustrations are in supporting a limited text. Children expect the picture to help them with their reading, especially when they encounter a new word. As soon as they hesitate, their eyes fly to the picture. Sometimes the illustrations in reading schemes are not as helpful and relevant as they might be. Sometimes they are even misleading. At one point in the 'Ladybird' scheme children read 'Peter and Jane look at the rabbit' when the text starts 'Peter and Jane look at the dog'. They should already know the word 'dog' from the earlier books in the series whereas the word 'rabbit' has not yet been introduced. The picture, however, shows Peter and Jane looking at rabbits. This classic error, which most children make, tells us a great deal about the way children read. It emphasizes their search for meaning which takes precedence over the literal text. It is also a test of teachers' attitudes. Some teachers will say to the pupil, 'Read what is there, not what you think ought to be there.'

Lower down the page in question Peter and Jane do

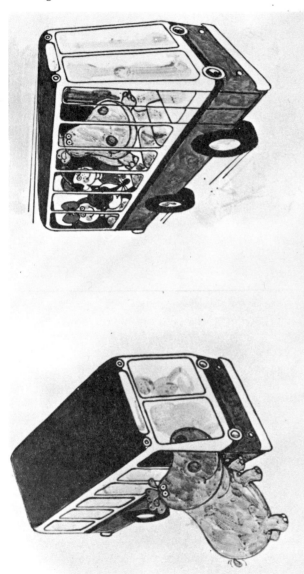

Then the bus went fast.

A hippopotamus got on the bus.

From *The Bus Ride* (Scott Foresman Reading System) published by Heinemann

'look at the rabbits' and this brings up the problem of picture-text ratio. The designers of reading schemes sometimes put in too much text alongside each picture. When illustrations are well done they can carry a large part, if not all, of the story line and so reduce the need for a large vocabulary.

The 'Laugh and Learn' series demonstrates the important point that the pictures in a reading book can tell the whole story, carrying the reader through the confines of a limited text which acts as a commentary or subtitling. The illustrations in *Watch Me* fully describe the humorous misadventures of Bushy, while the accompanying text uses only fourteen words, which are repeated between three and nineteen times.

Copious high quality illustrations are expensive. Publishers cannot expect to be thanked for charging a high price for their books but teachers and parents who criticize the cost should think in terms of value for money and the price they are willing to put on literacy. It would be a false economy to have fewer books with limited pictures and large slabs of text. Teachers who have used the old-fashioned reading books will know that a lot of children groan when they see a wedge of text unleavened by illustrations.

We have mentioned two important roles of illustrations: firstly to carry meaning, secondly to make the text less daunting. There are two other important functions of pictures: to make the book generally attractive and pleasurable to the child, and to draw him to the book in the first place. Once more, it is a question of what the child wants and needs, rather than what adults think he wants and needs. Teachers and parents tend to be rather subjective and often choose unsuitable styles. Children favour clarity of line and plenty of activity in their pictures. They have little taste for impressionistic and atmospheric pictures. Nor are children too bothered by fashion in illustrations.

Oh me, oh my.

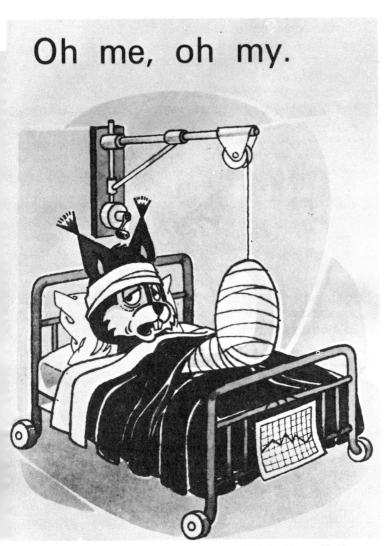

From *Watch Me* (Laugh and Learn series) by Terry Hall,
published by George Philip Alexander

Some attempts to bring their pictures up to date have been misguided and unnecessary. The 'Gay Colour' series has exchanged pleasant, simple outline drawings with few colours, for stylized blocks of colour, with which children seem less happy.

An art student carried out a fascinating experiment at our school. She illustrated various objects in different styles and asked the children for their preferences. The clearest, most representational and comic styles were favoured. Impressionistic versions were unpopular. A drawing by a prize-winning children's artist, which she also showed, was simply not understood.

By far the most popular illustrator for small children is Richard Scarry. His books stand on their illustrations alone and they are likely to be the childs' spontaneous selection from the bookshelves. Scarry's appeal lies in his depiction of ceaseless activity, and his wealth of meticulous and accurate detail. For example, he shows how things really work. Too whimsical for some teacher's tastes, he is nonetheless invaluable in showing that books can be enjoyed and learned from.

The only means a child has of seeing if a book is worth reading is the quality of the illustrations, and the jacket or cover illustration is the most important of all. This elementary fact is not always recognized by publishers. One otherwise attractive series of reading books used to have identical covers. The books languished on the shelves because the children were under the impression that they had read them before. The same series, with newly designed different covers, is now a great hit. I have looked at a whole range of what I know to be successful and popular early readers and found no single set of rules for illustrations. Many styles can be effective, including photographs, as long as pretentious and 'arty' pictures are avoided. Here are some examples of children's favourites: *Dominoes* has colour photographs; *Bangers and Mash,*

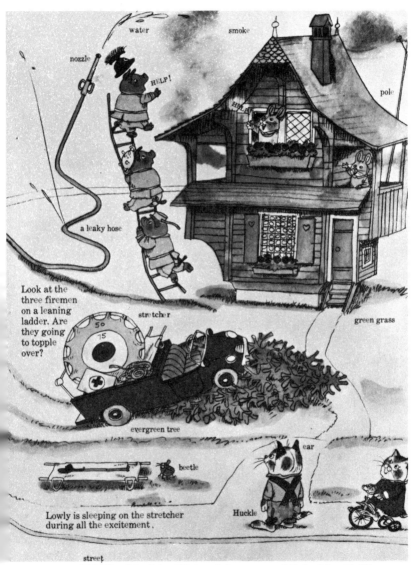

water

smoke

nozzle

HELP!

pole

a leaky hose

Look at the
three firemen
on a leaning
ladder. Are
they going
to topple
over?

stretcher

green grass

50

75

evergreen tree

ear

beetle

Lowly is sleeping on the stretcher
during all the excitement.

Huckle

street

From *ABC Word Book* by Richard Scarry, published by Collins

'Monster' books, the 'Laugh and Learn' series and *Oscar Rocket* all use comic drawings. On reflection it is hardly surprising that comic drawings come high on the list, since children like comics and cartoons so much. A whole range of comic styles is possible, from the sparse wit of Quentin Blake's monster to the uninhibitedly garish Oscar Rocket.

Ease of reading

We have already mentioned that unrelieved slabs of text are a deterrent to the young reader. Too thick a reading book also makes a child feel that reading is uphill work. Reading books should be short and sweet, preferably capable of being finished in a single session, giving a real sense of progress. Good layout and type smooth the reader's path. In a well-designed scheme, the print will be large and clear, with good spacing between letters and between words. The typeface used in the early stages will be close to the teacher's script, without serifs and other embellishments or distortions. Personally, I feel that children should get used to capital letters and normal punctuation from the start. It slightly slows down the learner to have to cope with two forms of each letter but, since he has to do it eventually, I see no point in postponing the issue, especially as the print a child will meet is not confined to a school reading book. Once children have started reading they show tremendous curiosity about all forms of printed messages.

A good scheme will use short sentences, each starting on a new line. This guides the beginning reader who is reading aloud and shows him where to stop and start again with 'a new voice'. The help that good layout can give to a reader is dropped too soon by most children's publishers. Even mature fluent readers can read more easily, and with more understanding, a piece that has been laid out for ease of reading rather than ease of printing – as the example

It is a well-worn platitude that the purpose of the printed word is to be read. This is a gross understatement. The purpose of all printing, whether of words or of pictures, is to communicate – ideas, information, instructions or emotions. The printed message should be not merely read but understood. Often its purpose is to spark off ideas or activities.

It is a well-worn platitude that the purpose of the printed word is to be read.
                 This is a gross understatement.

The purpose of all printing, whether of words
                              or of pictures,

    is to communicate – ideas,
                         information,
                         instructions
                      or emotions.

The printed message should be not merely read
                              but understood;

    its purpose is to spark off ideas
                        or activities.

From *The Visible Word*, by Herbert Spencer, published by Lund Humphries

reproduced on page 65, of so-called I.V.J. or internal vertical justification produced by Stefan Thermerson, shows.

First books should be written with short simple words that express simple and familiar ideas. Fluent adult readers can use text to predict the meaning of an unknown word – rarely do they have to use it to work out the sound. (Everyone has words in his vocabulary of which he knows the meaning but not the pronunciation.) Beginning readers have to read aloud, so they use the context to help them predict the sound of a new word as well as the meaning. It helps if they are guided towards the meaning of a word and are able to relate it to their own experience. Unfamiliar words and concepts should be kept to an absolute minimum. This may seem obvious but reading schemes and reading books are always being overtaken by cultural changes. For example, the 'Reading with Rhythm' series includes such words as 'black-smith' and 'sledge' which are unknown to many modern city children. On the other hand words such as 'cow' and 'dinosaur', although not in their direct experience, are culturally familiar through TV and picture books. As well as using familiar concepts, reading schemes should conform as much as possible to the rhythms of familiar language. For example, faced with the phrase, 'Peter has a ball' in the 'Ladybird' scheme children are as likely to read 'Peter has *got* a ball.'

Finally, one of the things that makes a book unattractive to children is when it has begun to look dirty and tattered. Books have to be bought with an eye as to how they will stand up to heavy use. In these inflationary times one cannot afford books that fall apart in the first few readings. Above all children like a new book that gives them a sense of getting on.

A sense of progress

The ideal reading system would be designed in imperceptible steps which ensured continuous progress. Unfortunately, most schemes have too steep a progression for the majority of average and below average children, with the result that there is always a sticking point. A child restricted to a particular scheme will come to feel that the way ahead is blocked. Frustrated readers can quickly become demoralized and the greatest enthusiasm can evaporate. Without a choice of material, when a reader gets stuck, there is no alternative but the indignity and boredom of starting again at some point. If this point is the beginning of a thick book the result can be disastrous – another argument for thin books. Children do not seem to mind reading a thin book again.

Even more telling is the argument for using several reading schemes in order to allow for sideways movement for slower readers and a variety of reading experience for everyone. However, a word of warning is necessary about any assumption that you can transfer a child from book three of one scheme to book three of another. The two schemes are unlikely to be strictly comparable, but even if they are of similar levels of difficulty, the vocabulary of the new scheme is probably so different from the original one that the child cannot cope with the unexpected vocabulary load. A far better course is to take the child back to the beginning of each new scheme and let him read through it fairly quickly. He then regains his confidence while meeting new words and getting ample opportunity for reinforcement of his existing vocabulary.

Startling differences in starting vocabularies

I have compared overleaf the starting vocabulary of three well-known reading schemes. Assuming a rough correspondence between the levels, there are some startling differences in the vocabulary sizes and frequency. What I have not shown, as being too complex, is the overlap of

	Scott Foresman	Ladybird	Laugh and Learn
level 1	BOOKS A-E	BOOKS 1a, 1b	BOOKS 1, 1a, 1b, 1c
total vocabulary	18*	16	67
total wordage	87	394	889
average number of repetitions	5*	22	13
level 2	BOOKS A-I	BOOKS 2a, 2b	BOOKS 2, 2a, 2b, 2c
total *new* vocabulary	263	27	151
total vocabulary	280	43	194
total wordage	1399	803	1645
average number of repetitions	5.0	1911	8.5

*There is also an alphabet book in this series which, included, will increase the total vocabulary to 52 and lower the total number of repetitions to 1.7.

vocabulary between schemes. (In fact, there is very little beyond extremely common words such as 'the', 'a', 'and', etc.) In any case, it will be plain from the different assumptions each scheme makes about what is a proper vocabulary load, that learner readers should not try to change horses in mid-stream. From the start 'Ladybird' goes all out for heavy repetition of a very small vocabulary. This follows from the philosophy of key words (the most frequently occurring words in the language which it is essential to know). The other two schemes have in common a much larger vocabulary with a lower repetition. 'Laugh and Learn' has an enormous wordage and the figures seem to suggest that there is a high rate of repetition. Of course, averages conceal as much as they reveal, and some of the words are repeated only once or twice – which does mean, however, that certain words have a frequency approaching that of the 'Ladybird' scheme.

The level 2 comparisons show a similar pattern although 'Scott Foresman' starts to move ahead of 'Laugh and Learn' in the number of new words introduced, while staying at its previous frequency of five words. Once more a close look at the distribution of this frequency shows that many words are used only once or twice.

'Ladybird' emerges from these comparisons as being the most tightly organized, offering the greatest likelihood of smooth progression based on constant repetition. The child may reach the end of level 2 with a vocabulary of only forty-three words but with a surer knowledge of them than children who have come across many times that number at the same stage in other schemes. A factor working against 'Ladybird' is that the so-called key words, although highly useful ones, are by their function uninteresting and difficult to illustrate. It may be as a result of the ultra-cautious approach of the first three stages that children tend to stall in the 'Ladybird' scheme on book 4, through a combination of too rapid introduction of new words and the boredom arising from the unexciting key word format. Nevertheless, these figures support the view that reading schemes such as 'Scott Foresman' and 'Laugh and Learn', which have a much less structured vocabulary, go too far in the other direction and risk being bewildering to a reader if they are used on their own. It is not the actual number of words that is the deterrent but the lack of repetition and of clues in the context and illustrations; above all, the critical factor is the ratio of familiar and unfamiliar words. A low vocabulary does not make for an easy book if a high proportion of these words are unknown. For example, the Dr Seuss 'Beginner Books' have a quite modest vocabulary of less than 150 words each, yet I put them at an advanced stage in my own 'banded reading scheme' because they have an individualistic vocabulary unrelated to any scheme or to each other. But this is jumping a little ahead.

Readability

The essence of any 'individualized reading' scheme is matching the readability level of reading books to the reading ability of children. This implies providing a wide variety of books, and being aware of the needs and interests of individual children. The concept of readability is not an abstract or statistical one. As Cliff Moon, whose scheme is probably best known, says, 'books are graded according to the ability of children to read them...the concept of readability...depends on the interaction between the reader and the text.' By 'interaction' he means listening to a child read from books and discussing the content of books he has read. So, using such practical criteria, he has built up comparative lists of selected reading books. Covering thirteen stages of reading, they incorporate many of the established reading schemes. Cliff Moon claims that individualized reading means that formal reading schemes are unnecessary, but he suggests that the ideas should be adapted for individual schools and classes. The broad scheme of individualized reading is as follows:

Stage	0	Pure picture books: the first reader
Stages	1,2,3	Introductory readers: caption books
Stages	4 to 10	Developmental readers
Stages	11,12,13	Bridging readers progressing from short to longer books, and on to general fiction, etc.

The rule that allows a child to move from one stage to another demands fluent reading of a variety of books at one stage, and the ability to read with an error rate of no greater than one word in twenty-five at the next stage. It is interesting to see how the reading schemes we have just compared are graded in Cliff Moon's *Individualized Reading*. The 'Ladybird' scheme does not figure at all. 'Scott Foresman' comes in at stage 1 with books A and B of the first level, and follows on with books C and D of level 1 and books A and B of level 2 in the second stage. 'Laugh and Learn' book 1 does not appear until stage 3 of 'individualized reading', and the rest of the 'Laugh and Learn' books are spread in sequence over stages 4 to 7, as are the other 'Scott Foresman' books, although not in the publisher's original order. Any teacher of reading will be fascinated by Cliff Moon's lists. They may disagree with individual titles but are likely to confirm the general logic of his choices.

Assessing new books

After all, it is not too difficult to work out criteria for deciding whether one book is easier than another for a beginning reader. The real problem is to decide at what stage of reading a book should be introduced, and in practical terms what set of books would be suitable for the particular age and ability range of the class. This facility, I fear, comes only from trial and error. The experienced teacher will have tried out enough books and will have found the sticking points for enough children at various stages of development, to decide where each book might fit in an individualized scheme. The new teacher must proceed with greater caution, both in creating an individualized reading scheme and making use of an existing one such as Cliff Moon's. She may be happier at first merging reading schemes into a rather simpler 'banded' programme. For a teacher whose classroom is rather short of

books and who may only have a limited number of
schemes, plus possibly a few library books, this is the only
tactic. Teachers are recommended to grade their reading
books according to criteria such as I have set out below. It
will help them evaluate reading books from the children's
point of view and to become expert in choosing new books.

Here are the questions I would ask in assessing a new
book:

1 Does it tell a story or is it otherwise sufficiently
interesting to be read aloud by the teacher and then by the
child?

2 Is the vocabulary compatible with regard to number
and familiarity of words?

3 Is the syntax helpful enough to allow the child to
anticipate and predict new words?

4 In particular, are the sentences short and well laid out
to assist punctuation?

5 Is there a suitable ratio of text to pictures for the
subject matter and age group?

6 Is the book short and easily finished?

7 Are the concepts in the book within the child's
experience and comprehension?

8 Is the text rhythmical and repetitive in an attractive
way?

9 Are the illustrations relevant and appealing in themselves?

The most effective way of making a book easier to read is
for the teacher to read it aloud to the children. This helps
with the context and gives clues to the difficult words, thus
'reducing uncertainty' – Frank Smith's phrase to describe
the mature reader's normal strategy.

Let us take the children's story in which the sky
fell on Chicken Licken. (A good version of this traditional
tale is published by Scholastic Book Services.) Here is an

ideal tale for telling aloud, and in the telling what might otherwise be difficult phrases such as 'Chicken Licken', 'Turkey Lurkey' and 'Foxy Loxy' become familiar. The language is highly repetitive, and thus far easier for a beginner than would appear at first sight. On this account I would give it a lower grading than other books of similar size and difficulty.

As I remarked earlier, problems arise when concepts and objects are beyond the children's ken. This is a fault of the otherwise well designed 'Reading with Rhythm' series which contains stories about such archaic things as copper kettles and blacksmiths, replaced in children's experience by the electric kettle and the garage mechanic.

'Non-book resources'

This is the jargon phrase that covers all kinds of material used in the teaching of reading, ranging from home-made games to elaborate audio-visual apparatus. They consist mainly of ancillary aids to reading, such as games and tape recorders, but there are also complete reading kits designed to take the place of reading scheme books. In this area, teachers must be particularly on their guard against extravagant claims by the manufacturers, and must have worked out very clearly what they expect from non-book resources. A comprehensive list of material available in this country has been produced by Bridie Raban. The booklet is called *Reading Skill Acquisition* and arranges the references in terms of four major levels: pre-literacy and beginning reading; early reading; word analysis and synthesis; and reading.

Games come in handy in making palatable the learning of dull or difficult words and phrases, putting over phonic and other rules and giving extra practice in vocabulary for slow learners and beginners. The changes can be rung on variants of familiar games. Children will play 'word bingo', 'word snap', 'word lotto', 'pairs' (some people know it as 'pelmanism') and never get bored, while practising words at a rate of repetition impossible to achieve in a book. To a certain extent children can play the simpler games themselves, and so learn without supervision, but this does not work for too long with the youngest children who cannot bear to lose. Repeated defeats for some children will soon lead to quarrelling and noisy behaviour. The teacher overseeing a game should see that nobody gets too frustrated and loses heart. A major drawback to games is that only a limited number of words can be taught, so their usefulness diminishes rapidly after the early stages simply because of the time and space they occupy compared with books. Nevertheless, every teacher can make good use of them as a pleasant and effective way of teaching the starting vocabulary of a reading scheme.

There are many commercially produced reading games, but some teachers enjoy making their own. Here are examples of two games devised by individual teachers. The first is a variation of word bingo, using pictures and shapes as well as words for the sake of simplicity and interest (suitable for a reception class). The second game uses simple but topical sentences, such as 'we like the snow' which the teacher writes on a piece of thin card. When the children have read the sentence several times the card is cut up into words. The children take it in turns to hide while one of the words is removed. When the child returns from hiding he has to say which word is missing. In this way useful phrases can be thoroughly and enjoyably learned. These games are of course, for children at the pre-reading stage; with caption books they provide an excellent preparation for beginning reading.

Tape recorders

The availability of relatively cheap cassette recorders and

tapes has encouraged their use in language teaching. There is a great variety of recorded material, some of it merely for listening to, some consisting of instructions, some of it complete in itself and some related to other printed material. The more pleasurable uses of tapes are usually also the more valuable. Tapes can introduce children to stories, poems, songs, and information at a higher level than they could get themselves from reading books, keeping children profitably occupied while the teacher is busy with a single child or a group.

Good quality tapes can also act as an incentive to children, familiarizing them with the potential value of books and allowing them to anticipate the pleasures of reading. The logical extension of simply listening for pleasure is a recording to accompany a reading book. For example, Penguin publish an excellent series of books and tapes called 'Listening and Reading' based on a B.B.C. programme. More didactic applications of tape recorders involve their use as a self-teaching device. A typical example of this is Bell and Howell's 'Language Master' system. The basis is a simple workcard with printed words and illustrations and a two-track recording tape. One tape carries the teacher's recording and the other enables the pupil to record and rerecord his own interpretation and to compare it with the teacher's. There are several programmes available as well as blank cards for the teacher to make up her own. They include such things as simple phonic exercises, support material for reading schemes, mathematics and language teaching. A similar device called the 'Card Reader' is available from Rank Audio-visual.

E.J. Arnold produce a teaching machine called the 'Audio Page' where a worksheet and a recording surface are ingeniously combined back to back. The worksheet is placed under a clear plastic overlay, on which the child can write with a water-based felt pen while receiving instruc-

tions through headphones. There are a number of programmes available covering such things as maths and
science as well as reading, plus blank sheets with which to
make your own. All equipment is extremely expensive,
right down to an electronic eraser at £33. It hardly seems as
versatile as work cards, ordinary cassette tapes, or even
good old pencil and paper – and a rubber.

Tape recorders and filmstrips related to story books and
other reading materials, such as those produced by Weston
Wood Studios, can be most attractive. To my mind
audiovisual teaching ceases to be fun and desirable when
the mechanics and the jargon take over from the teacher
and the child is turned into a sort of audiovisual receiver.

Pseudo-science

This dehumanizing aspect sometimes comes over most
strongly in so-called 'reading laboratories or kits'. The use
of such terms and a hyperbolic sales vocabulary give the
impression that all reading problems have yielded to the
power of technology. Woe betide the teacher who has not
realized this and is struggling along with old-fashioned
materials. If she were using the products of Science
Research Associates Ltd, she would, in the words of their
sales literature, be 'released for more individual work' and
could 'act as a learning consultant and curriculum plan-
ner'. Why carry on as a mere teacher in the light of such
promises? Might this be simply an excess of enthusiasm in
putting over the very latest methodology? Teachers with
£20 to £100 to spare can get one of these programmes and
see for themselves whether the material lives up to the sales
claims. In my opinion the typical content of the nicely
printed material is worthy but dull, verging on the old-
fashioned – certainly not as good value as the same money
invested in personal choice of books and equipment.

The 'laboratories' that I have studied betray their

American origins in the impressive packaging, the awe-inspiring labels ('Thinklab', 'Newslab', 'Learning Wheels', 'Listening Game Grids'), and the tendency to call spare coloured pencils 'replacement components'. Behind all this merchandizing are some very unrevolutionary work cards, comprehension exercises and reading booklets. Most of it is to an acceptable standard but might lose its appeal to teachers if it were presented simply as the latest collection of English exercises plus coloured pencils all the way from Chicago. I picked out at random a 'power builder' suitable for seven-year-olds. It consisted of a short biography of Friedrich Froebel, comprehension questions and phonic exercises. This is hardly riveting stuff for seven-year-olds, and reminded me of exercises I did in primary school many years ago. It is the kind of thing that will keep children occupied, in itself no bad thing, but a long way from its scientific pretensions. There is some irony in learning of Friedrich Froebel, who invented the kindergarten, that he 'made school a happier place for little children' after his own unhappy experiences at school, where 'he sat on a hard chair' and 'all day long he looked at books. The books had no pictures. Friedrich couldn't play. He couldn't do things with his hands. He had to sit in that hard chair and look at books. It was no fun.' I somehow don't think that Friedrich would have approved of the rigid and relentless reading laboratories.

Another well-known kit is the 'Stott Programmed Reading Kit', which consists of phonic exercises and games. The programmed aspect is the grading of the games in order of difficulty. The games themselves are a very pleasant way of teaching phonics but, like so many educational devices from the United States, the accompanying literature makes extravagant, pseudo-scientific claims for humble materials of the type that teachers have been devising and using for years. Teachers often use this kit as a supplement to their own reading programme. I mention

Stott in particular, as the Bullock Report found that no less than thirty per cent of schools were using it. Bullock also mentions that reading laboratories of one kind or another are used in twenty-five per cent of all primary schools. The likelihood of these devices being used increases with the age of the children. For instance, reading laboratories are favoured by merely nine per cent of infants-only schools, while the figure rises to forty-six per cent of junior-only schools.

This rather gives the game away. These laboratories are a convenient source of good old-fashioned comprehension exercises. The Bullock Committee's verdict on workshops and laboratories was as follows:

> In our view exercises in English text books or in kits of one kind or another are inadequate for developing comprehension. They provide too restricting a context and do not take account of the fact that reading should satisfy some purpose on the part of the reader. This may be to derive pleasure, experience or information: it may be serious, or it may be relatively trivial. But whichever it is, the individual will read most rewardingly when he has a personal reason for reading, for he will then carry his own attitudes and values into the text and not simply respond passively to it. The declared 'purpose' of so many of these exercises is to improve particular skills of comprehension. But even if there is any such result the improvement is so specific to the situation that it is unlikely to transfer to other reading tasks.

I have talked about games, kits and other non-book devices with regard to learning to read. Similar games and kits have been devised for the purpose of developing 'oral language', so called to distinguish it from written language. To me, the whole question of language development is important enough to justify a general discussion in another chapter. My view on reading games and such is that they should not be in lieu of books and book money should not be spent on them; but they can be used in the early stages of reading to reinforce basic vocabulary and later on to pep up flagging slow readers and backsliders.

Reading materials that parents can buy

Reading material produced for schools is not usually available in bookshops. Publishers vary in their attitudes. Some discourage sales to the general public, others put out special editions. However, in my opinion parents should think twice before subscribing to a reading scheme for their children. The one that most parents are likely to get is the 'Ladybird' series, because it is the most easily available and the most temptingly presented. The progression of 'Ladybird' books through 1a, 1b, 1c, to 2a, 2b, and 2c and so on seems straightforward, yet this scheme possesses the major drawback that comes from relying on a single reading scheme. Each of the numbered steps represents six months of reading age. For example 1a and 1b are for children with a reading age of four and a half, 2a and 2b for a reading age of five, and so on up to 12a and 12b which require a reading age of ten.

A bright child can be quickly taught the handful of words in the first 'Ladybird' reading books and once he knows them he can read 'Ladybird' 1a and 1b well inside an hour. Is he now supposed to mark time for another six months? Of course, he may be able to go straight on to books 2a and 2b. Sooner or later, however, most children will get stuck. The vocabulary load will become too much for them. They may enjoy rereading their old books several times over but not for six months at a stretch. Parents who are not aware of the timing of the scheme may become exasperated and disappointed at the child who is, apparently, slowing down. They may start to nag him just when he has become discouraged, and risk losing his interest in reading. It is understandable that some teachers disapprove of parents teaching their children to read with the aid of a reading scheme or otherwise in a plodding, insensitive way. Teachers may have to pick up the pieces.

It is much more difficult to get a child interested in reading who has been put off by an over anxious parent than one for whom reading is another exciting novelty at school. It is, of course, perfectly acceptable for parents to buy formal reading schemes with the blessing and co-operation of the teacher. I hope that I have not implied that teachers resent parents' efforts or regard them as competitors. Any teacher worth her salt will be delighted with a parent willing to get a child interested in books and even able to read before school. What counts is an awareness of the child's mood and enthusiasm. The moment a child starts to lose interest, reading should be set aside and given a rest. Many children will not be psychologically ready to read until after they have started school and there is plenty of time to help them.

I feel that parents are best advised to use the 'language experience approach' to reading. The methodical book by book approach should only be used after the child has started school and with the guidance of the teacher. Parents should look out for books with limited and controlled vocabulary so long as they have interest and appeal for the child. Such books will not automatically guarantee progress but they can be used either to help a child learn to read or quite simply as picture story books to be read aloud to the child.

A shopping list of books

For the teacher the parent is in an enviable position by being able to read books of all kinds and at all levels of difficulty, some of which will become favourites. Young children like to have their favourite book read to them over and over again. The parent can capitalize on this pleasure and gently guide the child into reading by pointing to the words as he goes. Children often learn books off by heart to the point of appearing to read them well enough to fool a casual observer. This is a commendable achievement and to be encouraged. With all of this in mind I have compiled a list of books that parents can buy at reasonable prices, capable of acting as picture reading books for children and reading aloud books for parents.

Dick Bruna's simplest books: *I Can Read, I Can Read More* and *My Vest is White,* published by Methuen.
Breakthrough books (published by Puffin): varied and interesting picture books with only a few words to each picture.
'Ladybird 563' series which include such titles as *The Party, The Zoo, Telling the Time, Going to School* and others (they have nothing to do with the Ladybird reading scheme).
'Little Nippers': the simplest end of the Nipper series (published by Macmillan), with plenty of slice-of-life humour.
Collins's 'Beginner Books', the famous series edited by Dr Seuss, with a zany, irrepressible style and comic illustrations, fully deserving their popularity with children.
Olga da Polga: the simplified version for beginning readers; the adventures of a guinea pig, written by Michael Bond, the inspired author of the 'Paddington Bear' series (published by Longman).
'Monster' books: the adventures of a friendly monster, with witty drawings by Quentin Blake (published by Longman).

'Well Loved Tales' and 'Read it yourself,' two series of simplified traditional stories by Ladybird. The latter are much the easier, but with a great deal lost in the simplification.

Nursery rhyme books in numerous versions: ideal material because children never tire of reciting rhymes and would be proud to be able to read them.

If you do not find any of the above recommended books in your local bookshop your bookseller will be willing to order them for you. My list is by no means exclusive, and it is not intended as a sort of substitute reading scheme; the books are meant to be read together by parents and children and they are of varying difficulty. For example Bruna's books are in stage 2 of Cliff Moon's 'Individualized Reading' list, while *Olga da Polga* is in stage 9. Other children's books are listed in Chapter 14 under *Favourites* and in the bibliography at the back.

4 Good Classroom Practice

Reading needs most organizing

> There are fifty children. It seems strange that I should have fifty to teach when all the time there are teachers with nobody to teach.... I go to the desk and open it to look for the register. Apart from the register there are only two other articles in the desk – a Bible and a strap!...Meanwhile the fifty sit in 'galleries' and sum me up as if I were a performer at a show. The gallery arrangement gives a good view of the teacher who is at the bottom of the slope in a position of strategic unimportance. This however is counterbalanced by the provision of a 'high' desk, and a chair where I can perch like a judge on the Bench. The wooden steps of the galleries are rough and the wooden floor is rough. The desks are dual desks and are clamped to the floor with iron stanchions...

Such were the layout and facilities of a typically formal classroom not quite fifty years ago as described in *Penny Buff* by Janetta Bowie. This delightful autobiography of a Clydeside infants teacher in the thirties shows that, while some things have changed dramatically, there is one thing in teaching that has not changed at all – human nature. However, the physical difference in today's primary classroom strongly influences the way reading is taught.

In the informal classroom of today you are likely to find

movable tables and chairs, working areas, such as a carpeted book corner, a science table, painting easels, and so on. If there is risk of clutter there may not even be individual places. So we have something of a paradox. Whereas yesterday children were arranged in an individual fashion and taught collectively, today they are arranged in a collective fashion and taught individually. This puts the controversy about formality and informality into perspective. Critics of the new freedom in primary schools have claimed (more emotively than statistically) that it has produced a decline in reading standards. However, any risk to reading standards in informal methods has nothing to do with informality as such but with the way it is interpreted. For an informal classroom to work well, a great deal of planning is required. Within it, reading needs the most organization.

Janetta Bowie had to hand out fifty identical reading primers and then collect them all at the same time – this is done whether they can all read the first one or not. Each child was tested at set times.

The children each stand up, holding the beginners' reader in both hands. Those who desperately want to point to the words are completely frustrated.... I do wish Miss Monroe would let them sit down with the book on the desk. Merely watching them, I become as fidgety as the children. I am quite sure that Miss Monroe does not read the books and newspapers at home, standing up.

The arithmetic of teaching time

Present-day teachers are more considerate. Children work with their own books at their own speed and their progress is measured in a more relaxed way. As we have seen, with individualized reading we have the complete antithesis of the traditional whole class method. Yet the new way makes far greater demands on the school's most precious commodity, teaching time. The class teacher's problem is fitting the needs of thirty children into a five-hour day. It seems a lot when it is converted into three hundred minutes, but it means a maximum of ten minutes of individual tuition for all subjects. When playtime, assembly, milk time, class lessons such as P.E., music, and story time are taken away, five minutes a day on average would be nearer the mark. A teacher intent on helping each child individually must plan ahead. She must work out in detail how she is going to spend each day, organize the classroom meticulously, and must make sure of arriving each day well before the children in order to have everything prepared for them. Even then the need remains for some class and group teaching in order to make the most efficient use of the teacher's time.

Let us go back for a moment to the clash of wills between Miss Bowie and Miss Munroe. The latter

is annoyed that the children in my class can scarcely be heard when they stand up to read aloud. I reply that good reading is a matter of understanding and not elocution. I confess to bringing them out to read to me individually, so that each one reads at his own level and rate. She is not at all in sympathy with this. 'That takes too long. They should read round the class, and everybody gets a chance.' 'Only about two lines,' I say, 'the other way they can read a page!' 'They should learn to keep the place, too,' she says. I remember my own school days, when 'keeping the place' reduced me to a nervous wreck, and keeping the place was more important than what the story meant. 'The slow ones can't do it,' I say. 'We all must do it the same way in the Infant Department' are her last words.

The need for fewer, longer reading sessions

Today I would criticize as poor practice the idea of children reading only one page at a time to their teacher. I would ask adults what they think they would get out of reading a novel at the rate of a page a day. Reading in a fragmented way is frustrating at any level. I recommend that children read a whole story at a session, even though this means that the teacher will only manage to hear each child read about once a week. The benefits of a long uninterrupted reading session include more enjoyment from following the story, more sense of achievement, and a better model of what reading constitutes. We have seen how difficult it is, especially in the early stages, to guarantee meaning with a limited vocabulary. Chopping up a story into short pieces of prose will make it even harder to follow. If children's attitudes to reading are formed by working through disconnected slices of text is it any wonder that the majority of children come to dislike books, and take no pleasure in *sustained* reading?

If children are allowed to read only a page at a time most of the value of built-in repetition is lost. The more the child reads on, the more chance there is of repeated words being committed to memory. But any break, however short, both slows down learning and increases the chance of forgetting again. Over a long session the teacher can see if the repeated words are becoming familiar and can judge fluency, especially in those children who do take some time to 'warm up'. Finally, a practical benefit from fewer, longer sessions is the time saved. It always takes a minute or two to call children, to get them to find their book and their place and then to record what they have achieved. I have found that the greatest advantage of a longer session is that children become gripped by the story in exactly the same way as an adult becomes gripped by an exciting story and insists on finishing it to find out what happens. This will bring forward the time when children will happily read to themselves and so proves a good investment of the teacher's time. While recommending a lengthy session once a week for most children, I feel that more frequent practice has to be made available for two sets of children: the very slowest readers who seem to forget their words quickly, and the absolute beginners. Both these groups lack the critical 'starter' vocabulary that enables a learner reader to pull himself up by his bootstraps by inferring new meanings from the context. Fortunately, there is no more than a handful of such children at any one time.

In the beginning, children prefer to read to other people rather than to try to read aloud by themselves. Therefore, although the child will learn best from an intensive period with the teacher perhaps once a week, ideally this should be supported by as many other listeners as possible. Everyone can help – parents, older brothers and sisters, neighbours, friends, uncles and aunts. Some schools have volunteer parents who come in to hear children read. Others use ancillary helpers. An especially valuable source of listeners is a local secondary school, whose children will help as part of their community service.

Reading in groups

I have described the ideal state of affairs where children learn to read as individuals with their own range and sequence of books, enjoying the individual tuition of the teacher. Some teachers feel forced to compromise through lack of time and this usually leads them towards group reading. The usual practice is to choose children of about the same reading ability who will read aloud from identical books in turn, while the rest are meant to follow the text silently with their eyes. This is not much of an advance on reading round the class. The same drawbacks apply. Although beginning readers need to read aloud, and can learn from other children's mistakes, they are just as likely to become frustrated and lose interest, 'switching off' until it is their turn to read. In effect they are getting a fraction of the apparent reading practice and would be better off reading individually. There is a danger of group reading sessions lapsing into a dull chore. In particular, they may hold back a bright child ready to forge ahead on his own. When group performance dominates, the hardest working members of the group are inevitably kept to the pace of the slowest. The only successful way of organizing reading groups is to have one member reading to the teacher while the rest get on with independent practice such as reading simple books alone, preferably books that they have read before and know so well that they do not require the teacher's help. This is a much more successful strategy than preparing a page to read to the teacher where a lot of the teacher's help will be required.

Whether the teacher is concentrating on individuals or groups, the practical problem arises of what the rest of the class should be doing. Their activities need to be absorbing but simple enough for them not to need the teacher's constant help, and quiet enough not to distract the reader.

For very young children, play is the answer, preferably with free choice activities such as classroom toys, sand and water play, painting, drawing and tracing, and playing in the Wendy House. The point about these activities is that they carry their own rewards and satisfactions. The alternative to them is simple, formal work, such as practice with letters and numbers, work cards, word matching and so on. With very young children such study can be demanding on the teacher as it requires a lot of supervision and encouragement, thus defeating the object of freeing the teacher to concentrate on hearing reading. As children get older and are able to concentrate for longer periods, they can settle down to more formal exercises. Whatever the activities chosen, they must be well organized. A child must know where to find everything he needs. Any tasks should be well within his capacity, so that he does not feel the need for the teacher's advice and support, and they should be self-checking. All in all this is a time for consolidation and practice of established skills. To keep children occupied, interested and learning in this way, calls for varied materials to be applied with imagination in a well ordered classroom, and for a high degree of planning and preparation.

How much time should be spent on reading ?

This question can best be answered by another one. Is there anything more important than being able to read? Reading has to take the lion's share of time until children have the benefit of being able to learn other subjects by reading. It is practically impossible for children to make progress in primary mathematics, science, environmental studies, and so on without the ability to read printed instructions and information. And even more obviously, you have to be able to read your own writing. All this would be platitudinous but for the fact that some children reach secondary school unable to read at all or to read well enough to cope with print. Recently a Schools Council survey confirmed fears that a majority of children never look at another book once they leave school (*Children and Their Books,* by Frank Whitehead). I believe that all children could learn to read with individual tuition. As we saw in the chapter on reading theory, the reading teacher's art is to teach a child to teach himself to read. This is better done in sustained periods of reading help than in snatches. So we can calculate what proportion of the average school week needs to be devoted to reading when children are in the learning stage.

A primary school week is between twenty-five and twenty-eight hours. If a teacher of a class of thirty gave each child a fifteen-minute session this would take up seven and a half hours – in practice about two school days' worth of time. This seems a reasonable minimum. I feel that between thirty per cent and forty per cent of class time should be given over to teaching reading until children have become fluent, confident and able to carry on by themselves. However, when this happy point is reached, the teacher would be ill-advised to give up hearing children read all together – some children would lose interest and cease to make progress. Oddly, most books on learning to read do not go into this matter.

Good work seen but not heard

Joan Dean's estimate in the B.B.C. publication *Teaching Young Readers* is similar to mine. She says, 'Most teachers of young children probably devote about a quarter of the total time on language work, although it will in another sense be part of all the work children are doing.' Yet some teachers are horrified at my estimate. They would happily allocate a greater portion of time to writing, because it appears to be more productive work, with plenty to show at the end of it; because, frankly, listening to children read can become quite tedious; and because by not giving reading priority they run short of time.

These attitudes were well illustrated by a student teacher of my experience. She worked very hard. She grouped the children and set them various written tasks. After some time I pointed out that she had still not heard any children read. She said she was worried about it but just hadn't had time. This was perfectly true as she conscientiously spent all her time guiding and helping the children, explaining instructions and giving spellings. I suggested that because this age group was so demanding of teacher's time when doing written work, she should let them play while she heard reading. She replied that she couldn't possibly allow that since they would shortly become juniors and the junior head would be displeased if they did not have a good work habit. True as that might be, I felt he would be more displeased if they could not read.

Although I have stressed the importance of individual reading, there has to be some class teaching simply to fit everything in that has to be learnt. Fortunately, there are some things that lend themselves to full class instruction. For example, the teacher can use short class sessions to introduce and familiarize particular books that the children will read; to make general teaching points such as explaining punctuation; to show flash cards; to teach phonic rules and spelling rules. The last three items are probably best incorporated into a game such as a quiz or I-Spy.

5 Getting Started

Hard-working words

The most devout supporters of the phonic method of teaching would allow that the best means of getting children started with reading is to have them looking at and saying commonly used words, the words that anyone must know in order to read the simplest English. As we shall see, there is some disagreement about precisely which words are used most, but the general principle remains that a small number of words accounts for a staggeringly large proportion of our speech and writing. American researchers have estimated that only fifty words account for over half the volume of our spoken language. W. Murray and J. McNally, the authors of *Key Words to Literacy,* upon which the 'Ladybird' reading scheme is based, give a key word list of 250 words which they say accounts for 73.3 per cent of the words in juvenile reading. Another way of looking at it is that certain words work so hard in the language that they appear every few words. For example the words 'the', 'of', 'and', or 'to' appear as every sixth word in a piece of normal English prose. (You may like to see for yourself by counting the frequency of these words so far in this chapter.)

It is the beginning reader's misfortune that these words in our language, which have been aptly called 'carrier' words, are often ones where the written and spoken forms have diverged considerably. Edwards and Gibbon, in their book *Words Your Children Use,* estimated the popularity of words used by infant children in their writing. The most frequently used words include many which are phonic stumbling blocks or are inconsistent between themselves. For example the words 'to' and 'go' are both irregular and inconsistent. The word 'to' is not to be confused with 'too' and 'two'. 'I' and 'my' both have the sound 'i'. The words 'some', 'have', 'are' and 'one' all have unexpected spellings. 'Is' is not 'iss'; it is 'iz'.

I use the word 'there' to show infants some word magic. Take away the 't' and you have 'here'. Take away the last letter and you have 'her'. Take away the 'r' and you have 'he'. Add back the 't' and you have 'the'. Which can be 'the' as in 'the apple' or 'the' as in 'the teacher'. You can see how confusing it all is, and why flash cards are useful for teaching these so-called 'sight' words. But even words that are phonically regular cannot be learned phonically until the appropriate rule has been taught. Therefore flash cards are necessary to teach a starter vocabulary of such words as 'make', 'made' where the final 'e' modifies the 'a'; words like 'look', 'see' with their double vowels, words like 'little' where the double consonant shortens the 'i', and many more, until you are in the position I described in the first chapter where you would otherwise have to learn 166 rules before actually starting to read.

Now let us consider how flash cards work. In spite of their name they are rarely 'flashed'. The normal practice is to show the flash card – a card on which a single word is printed in large lower-case letters – for a few seconds, asking children to look at it carefully. Depending on whether they are new words or not, the children can be told what they are, or asked to recognize them. Repeated presentation and telling ensures that the children will learn them. Yet the process whereby learning takes place is not as elementary as it seems. When a child learns to recognize a word on a flash card, the teacher cannot be certain just what features of it he is using to distinguish it from other

words in the set. Every teacher is familiar with the child
who learns to identify a flash card word not by the word
itself but by some accidental feature of the card, such as a
smudge or broken corner. It is harder to observe exactly
which and how many identifying features of the word the
child is using.

Easy words like 'aeroplane' and 'chocolate'

This point is worth dwelling on because teachers can be
disappointed to find that children are unable to recognize
in another setting, words they seem to know perfectly well
on flash cards. Let us take the example of a beginning
reader who confuses the words 'horse' and 'here'. He may
be making too economical a choice of identifying features,
perhaps the beginning and end letters and the general
similarity of the two words. At the other end of the scale a
long and apparently difficult word in a set of flash cards
may be picked up with astonishing ease. In the starter
vocabulary of the 'Janet and John' reading scheme the
word 'aeroplane' is perhaps the quickest to be learned. It is
often pointed out that it is an interesting and emotive
word. At the same time it is by far the longest and most
unusual word in the set. I have demonstrated the same
principle with an audience of adults: in order to give them
an idea of what it is like to begin reading, I use flash cards
of Russian words in Cyrillic script. Whereas the boring
everyday words are hard to memorize, the long – and
interesting – word for chocolate is recognized without fail
at the second showing.

   All of this shows that learning to read is chiefly a process
of visual trail-and-error, by which the distinctive features
are built up for each word with which a child becomes
familiar. If making mistakes and guessing are treated as
carelessness and faults, the child's learning will be slowed
down. The other thing we can be sure of is that the sooner

words are encountered in a clear context, the more the correct feature list will be built up and the more swiftly they will be applied. A child would not make the mistake of reading that 'the cowboy jumped on his here'.

A beginning reader ought to meet the words of his first vocabulary in as many settings as possible. This can be achieved by such techniques as word-to-word matching, where, for example, a flash card can be matched to a wall caption or where a sentence cut up into separate words is reassembled alongside a whole version. Other ways of familiarizing children with words are tracing, copying and making them with plasticine.

The varied forms of letters

Adults are so used to reading that they overlook the way the same word, even a simple word, can vary considerably in the details of its shape – i.e., in the distinctive features that the child so painfully learns. Here are five printed versions of the words 'cat' and 'dog' which visually could be from different languages.

cat	DOG
cat	Dog
CAT	Dog
Cat	dog
Cat	dog

We are so accustomed to these variations that we probably do not notice that the form **dog** is less like **DOG** than it is like **bag** or **day**. Aware of this kind of confusion, teachers may go to great lengths to ensure that children are presented with only one form of script. Capitals may be frowned on and teachers adapt their own handwriting to a simple, rounded, unadorned, print style.

Yet I feel this can go too far. It seems to me better for children to meet the varied forms of letters quite early on. It may slow down their initial learning but will pay dividends later. For children are very inquisitive about words and will try to read them wherever they are encountered: as signs, labels, titles on the television screen, advertisements, notices and so on. It could be argued then that a beginning reader does not 'know' and cannot 'read' the word 'dog' until he has come across all its possible forms.

Caption books

The technique I have come to favour for getting children started in reading is the use of caption books as 'instant readers'. Caption books are fairly widely used as practice reading for a child who can read. They are not used as much as they might be with absolute beginners. Caption books have been described as 'flash cards in book form'. Usually they have the additional advantage of an illustration which rings the changes on an unvarying basic phrase. A typical example is *This is my Colour* by Derek and Lucy Thackray, which I described earlier. Once a child knows what the master phrase says and realizes he can guess the object from the illustration, he has become an instant reader. He is very like the learner who can swim with the aid of water wings. Once words are seen in their context, the risk of confusion is considerably reduced. When a child can correctly point to each word as he is saying it, he has begun to read. At the same time he is picking up the conventions of written language, such as reading from left to right and top to bottom, turning over the pages, and reading in sequence from front to back. He becomes accustomed to the spaces between written words. We are so used to them that we forget there are no such spaces between the spoken words of a sentence. To my mind, this early caption book work effortlessly disposes of the argument for separate training in left to right eye movements and other visual gymnastics.

By having several sets of different caption books to hand a teacher can keep beginners 'reading' for as long as necessary before starting a formal reading scheme. This is better than teaching the children the words in their first reading book before letting them move on to it. A few children can be in infant school for as long as two years before they are ready to read. They would soon become aware of their failure to get their first primer, and slip into the role of backward readers. Such loss of confidence is avoided when the slower readers are continually reading caption books. There is no clear division between those who can and cannot read. The variety of books prevents the boredom that comes from repeated failure with a single reading scheme.

Removing the mystique from reading readiness

An important side benefit of using caption books in the way I have described is that it removes the mystique from the notion of 'reading readiness'. Caption books anticipate and prepare for reading without requiring a magical moment when suddenly a child can read properly. It used to be believed that children's readiness to read was bound up with their physical and mental development – their 'maturation'. The shorthand for this notion was that children learned to read at the age of six. The effect of such thinking was to persuade teachers not to bother with reading until children were six or until they showed unmistakable signs of 'reading readiness', such as showing an interest in books or demonstrating powers of concentration. A teacher might believe that it was pointless to teach an 'immature' child the rudiments of reading. In one class I came across a child who impressed me with his attention in story-telling and his intelligent questions, even though he was in other respects babyish and unruly. The teacher was unwilling to start him on reading but when I tried him with a few flash cards, the first time I repeated a word he said, 'You've shown me that one before'. I realized that if he could recognize a word so quickly he was obviously ready to read. Within a few weeks he was an accomplished reader.

Pre-reading skills

People became sceptical of the idea of reading readiness depending on maturation because it seemed to imply that whatever the teacher did, a child's ability to read could not be brought forward. The desire to bring reading readiness under the control of the teacher has led to the growth of an unfortunate modern practice. Reading readiness is seen as the culmination of training in skills such as those mentioned earlier: vocabulary and language development; visual and auditory discrimination; language growth; sequential thinking; and left–right eye movements.

Training for such skills is built into preparatory programmes culminating in a battery of 'reading readiness tests'. These tests are used on a large scale in the United States and it is my impression that they are gaining ground in this country. It is a neat idea – it removes guesswork, and one can see its appeal for teachers. They can be advised exactly when to start a child reading. Derek and Lucy Thackray have produced a programme which leads to the 'Thackray Reading Readiness Profiles', covering the skills detailed above. I have tested scores of children of varying reading ability at different stages in their progress and I have found no correlation between their reading ability and their performance on the reading readiness profiles. In extreme cases, some fluent readers failed dismally.

Thus I have yet to see any validation for reading

readiness tests. The Thackrays themselves admit, 'the "Thackray Reading Readiness Profiles" have not been designed to tell a teacher when a child is ready or not for reading...even so the results will indicate quite clearly those children who are strong in all the reading readiness measures...and also those children who are weak in all the measures...' It seems to be another of those tests that find out which children are good at taking tests. In terms of teaching children to read, it is largely a waste of time. The best way of preparing a child for reading is to get him as close as possible to the real thing by giving him a well planned and varied programme of pre-reading activities, such as caption books, flash cards and reading games, story-telling and so on. He may not be at the point of 'reading readiness' for some time but if the programme is sensitively handled he will not get bored or frustrated, and ultimately he will learn to read, just as ultimately every child learns to speak. The point at which children do start to speak – their 'speaking readiness' – is usually about fourteen months of age. Nonetheless mothers talk to their babies from birth and we are now certain that this is part of the way that children learn to speak. Any mother who assumed that there was no point in talking to her child till he was fourteen months of age would definitely retard him.

Which words should a child learn first?

A school which bases its reading programme on only one or two schemes will set the children to learn the words they will meet in their first primer. One which does not limit itself in the reading schemes it uses will be faced with the problem of which words to concentrate on among the various basic vocabularies. It will probably be decided to teach first the most commonly used words. These are the words which will be encountered soon in any early reading material except a purely phonic programme. Users of the

'Ladybird' scheme will have their attention drawn to the 'key words' which make up a disproportionately large part of the language.

The best source for choosing words of most appeal and use to beginning readers is the reference book I mentioned earlier, *Words Your Children Use* by Edwards and Gibbon. The authors systematically examined the writing of young children of five, six and seven years and drew up comparative lists showing the order of popularity of words by children in the different age groups. Although in general the frequency of words used by children does not differ from that of words in general usage, there are telling differences in the order of popularity between different ages. For example, the word 'play' is so important to five-year-olds that it is fourth in the list after 'a', 'the' and 'I'. By the age of six it has dropped to eleventh and at seven years it is only the eighteenth most popular word. The word 'house' shows a similar movement, going from ninth among five-year-olds to twenty-first among six-year-olds, and to forty-sixth among seven-year-olds. There are plenty of fascinating insights in these lists and they raise two important questions which will be developed in a later chapter: how far does the language of early reading reflect children's own choice of language? To what extent does children's writing help their reading and vice versa?

Should you teach your baby to read?

Obviously the question of reading readiness is also likely to crop up with pre-school children. Precocious children can give irresistible signs of wanting to read. Parents may be eager to teach their children to read but may be aware of some vague hostility on the part of teachers. In 1963 Glenn Doman, an American doctor caused a sensation with his book *Teach Your Baby to Read*. In his experience with brain-injured children he had discovered that one-year-old babies could be taught to read, 'for if an arbitrary collection of sounds, formed into a word, could convey a meaning to a one-year-old why should it not be possible for an arbitrary collection of shapes to do the same?' The quotation is from Felicity Hughes, an English follower of Doman, who published *Reading and Writing Before School* in 1971.

Whatever you may think of the idea of baby bookworms, both books are well worth reading, written with good sense and humour, putting a plausible case for very early teaching of reading and dealing crisply with most of the objections to it, including the notion of reading readiness. There is no doubt that Doman and his followers have established the possibility and to a certain extent the attractiveness of teaching babies to read. But in their concern with the technique, they have not dealt with three major objections. The first is that a baby is a baby for such a short time that these precious months are surely better used in play, talk and cuddles. These must take precedence over any formal instruction, even if it is disguised, in the Doman method, as a game using what are in effect huge flash cards of important words such as 'Mummy' and 'Daddy'. This leads on to the second objection, that however adept a baby could become at recognizing words he would remain culturally incapacitated. He could not handle books. Very few written messages in his environment would be likely to mean anything to him. There is no suitable ready-made material. He would be physically incapable of writing. The argument is surely that we learn to read and write when the need arises – this need may express itself quite early on but only at a point when we find it useful and enjoyable to communicate facts and experience at a distance and over time. None of this is relevant to a baby who lives so close to his parents and has not the slightest interest in the abstract nature of written language. At the domestic hearth speech is a hundred times more efficient and satisfying. The final argument against teaching your baby to read is the risk of failure: for every Felicity Hughes or Glenn Doman who does it with warmth and joy there will be another parent who does it with anxiety and a sense of striving. The latter may be successful, but there is a risk, of which teachers are painfully aware, of putting children off reading books altogether.

As soon as children show that they are old enough to handle books and that they enjoy the printed word, there is no harm in a little incidental teaching, provided it is sensitively handled. The most valuable thing that parents can do is to get their child used to the pleasures of books by looking at picture books with him. If the text is suitably short and in large type they can point to the words while reading. If a child seems to learn words, that is all to the good, but if he doesn't then there is no need to worry. Another enjoyable way of getting children interested in reading is to make books together by cutting interesting pictures out of magazines, sticking them in a scrapbook or home-made book and providing simple captions. The same sort of thing can be done with children's drawings, either separately or in book form. If the intention is to try and teach reading, then the more repetitive the captions the better, in the style of the school caption books I described.

On the other hand, children may get more fun and benefit from seeing their own stories written down without artificial limitations. My own son drew pictures and dictated at speed long stories to accompany them. He loved hearing them read back over and over again but they would have been quite useless for the teaching of reading and writing. I think it is far better to aim at this sort of achievement than to try and anticipate school too much, where in any case the most devoted teacher cannot spare the time to act as amanuensis. The plain fact is that most children will learn to read when they go to school and the ones that are going to find it hardest and slowest are the ones who are least likely to learn as toddlers. While I would encourage parents to point out labels and names of things, I would discourage the use of flash cards at home. Indeed, I would not approve of a teacher showing flash cards to a single child – it is a far too dull and limited approach, whereas flash card games with a group of children make it palatable.

There is another worthwhile recommendation I can make to all parents: to teach their children the alphabet. For no good reason the alphabet has come to be seen as somewhat old-fashioned. It has to be learned by heart sooner or later with the shapes and identifying sounds of letters. What might be something of a task later on is for very young children great fun, with the aid of alphabet blocks, ABC books, and alphabet soup.

6 Making Progress

Fits and starts

There are emotional and practical reasons for knowing when a child becomes able to read but there is no easy way of defining it. As with 'reading readiness,' a certain amount of hindsight is often used when saying that a child can read. Each type of reading programme will obviously have different starting points. An old-fashioned phonic scheme, for example, requires the child to have learned the phonic rules at the back of the book before he can start reading the text. A more modern 'look and say' scheme will require children to have learned the vocabulary of the first book on flash cards before starting to read it. In order to try and give children a running start, teachers would want them to have learned two books' worth of flash cards. My own rule of thumb is for a child to be able to recognize in different contexts about twenty words, mostly of the useful 'carrier' type that occur so often in the language. Whichever philosophy of reading is employed, some priming of this sort will be necessary.

Children seem to fall into three groups in the manner in which they begin to read. One group learns its essential vocabulary, gets the hang of reading efficiently and will have started reading in its first school term. The middle group will take much longer to get started, even up to two years, but at some point everything seems to fall into place. Reading 'clicks' and smooth progress follows. The last group comprises the slower readers, who will take a long

104

time to learn their first words, and afterwards will always need a lot of help with their reading. However, we ought not to lose sight of the fact that parallel with learning goes forgetting. Holidays, illnesses, major distractions, such as a change of school, can seem to push a child backwards. All in all, there is no time when you can say with certainty that a child will make smooth progress in reading. It will appear to go in fits and starts. But all the time what is happening is a general build-up of vocabulary. Words are encountered in a variety of settings, some of them frequently, others rarely. This process goes on into adulthood. We never stop learning to read. For we are always coming across new words, and old words used in an unfamiliar way.

How the reading buck is passed

Once you see reading as a continuous development, as a tool that sharpens itself in use, it is hard to accept the notion that it is merely a set of physical skills. You see the need to teach reading with the goal of fluency throughout a person's education. Failure to understand this has meant a neglect of reading in the education system. It was once strongly believed that teaching reading was solely the province of the infant school, that children once given the means to 'crack the code' needed little further help, practice or encouragement. If a child in junior school could not read it was said to be the fault of the infant school, if a child in secondary school could not read it was the fault of the primary sector. If an army recruit could not read it was the fault of the education system. Yet if reading was seen as a developmental process rather than as the acquisition of a finite set of skills, this would never happen. Even now few secondary schools have reading lessons on the time-table, except for the remedial class, although by definition the average child entering a secondary school will have a reading age of eleven, which is not an adequate standard of literacy. Reading often becomes a mere accessory of the English department. Is it any wonder, when reading is seen as a decoding skill quite separate from the extraction of meaning, that other subject teachers fail to see what responsibility they have for teaching reading or how to set about it? Teachers who conceive of reading as a decoding process will see fluency as desirable but not essential because it is the demonstration that the child is reading for meaning. Children who are struggling hesitantly through a text do not understand what they are reading and if they are reading too slowly, their sensory and short-term memory will be blocked.

Fluency and comprehension

What then do I mean by fluency? I do not mean word perfect delivery or highly expressive reading. Fluency rests upon a certain smoothness, a reasonable speed and a tolerable rate of error. It would be useful to have a rule of thumb of what an acceptable rate of error might be, but little work seems to have been done. Cliff Moon suggests in *Individualized Reading* that 'an error rate no greater than one word in twenty-five' is the minimum fluency. Elizabeth Goodacre draws attention to various levels of reading ability measured by an American device called the 'Informal Reading Inventory'. Here the so-called 'independent level' involves not more than one mistake in twenty words, and the 'instructional level', i.e., with the teacher helping the child, not more than one in ten. A 'frustration level' occurs when more than one word in ten is misread (quoted in *Teaching Young Readers,* a B.B.C. publication).

Moving gradually from the known to the unknown

These ratios seem plausible. What they suggest is that,

depending on the circumstances and the material, between ninety and ninety-six per cent of the words strongly indicate the meaning of the remainder. If the proportion of unknown words becomes too great for the context, meanings become blurred. Misunderstandings about this balance between familiar and unfamiliar words in the crucial stage of building a vocabulary can lead teachers into separating comprehension and reading skills. I have heard a teacher say. 'He can read but he has no comprehension.' There are programmes designed to teach comprehension skills in their own right. There are tests designed to measure 'pure' comprehension.

I do not regard it as a sign of my inability to read that I fail to comprehend my income tax form. The fault is surely with the writer. He has not even met me half way. His explanations and clarifications make me more confused than ever. But ignorance of his obscure phrases will be no excuse. Dealing with officialese I begin to understand how a small child feels who is given something to read which is beyond this 'comprehension'. The fault must lie with the teacher. If teaching someone to read is gradually feeding him a controlled diet of unknown words to add to his store of known words it is absured to overburden him with slabs of fresh knowledge. Reading material by definition must be comprehensible. If it is not, it is wrong for that child. For a child to comprehend a piece of prose it must be within both his reading ability and his knowledge and experience. The learner reader should move very gradually from the known to the unknown.

Ninety per cent of the art of teaching reading

The teacher should ease the path of the learner by introducing the reading material, familiarizing it, and if necessary, explaining it. Even teachers who are alert to this sometimes overlook the boundaries of children's knowledge and assumptions. This is especially true where children come from different cultural backgrounds or have very narrow environments. A typical example is a popular reading scheme, the Griffin 'Pirate' series, originally designed for juniors, which is so attractive that it is often used with infants. Yet many of them have no inkling of what 'p-i-r-a-t-e-s' or 'i-s-l-a-n-d-s' or 's-a-i-l-s' are. It greatly helps therefore to provide a useful and exciting introduction to the vocabulary by telling stories about pirates, making maps and models of islands, drawing and modelling boats with sails, and so on. The final, logical step is to read the books first to the children.

I want to dwell on this simple suggestion to read the books beforehand to the children because I think it is crucial to the success of teaching reading. First, consider the valuable test that this entails. If there is material which the teacher finds herself unable and/or unwilling to read to an audience of children it is probably by this definition unsuitable material for learning to read. It can be unreadable because a) it is simply too boring, too flat, uneventful, unvarying and generally lacking in any pace or drama – this goes for many reading schemes; b) it is beyond the child's intellectual and emotional level – there may be words, concepts, facts, feelings, styles that remain beyond his grasp; c) it may be suitable in other ways but too long and drawn-out for the child's short span of attention. If children are given tedious or otherwise unsuitable reading matter they may read dutifully and mechanically, switching off from any real understanding. Recently I watched a child being given a reading test by a research student. I was most interested in how he would get on. In spite of that I found myself switching off. This might be a surprise to those unfamiliar with the stilted and archaic language of such tests, e.g.

The stricken submarine lay at a depth of approximately one hundred and twenty feet. Although it was common knowledge that the treacherous currents of the area would make rescue operations difficult, the crew remained disciplined and confident. Meanwhile...a diver with technical equipment for their release was in peril. His life-line had become entangled around a projection on an adjacent wreckage. Experience warned him against his first impulse to dislodge the line by force .

When it came to the comprehension questions I found that I could not have answered them because I had listened without taking in a word. I had an awful glimpse of a world where children read without understanding to teachers who listen without hearing.

Ninety per cent of the art of teaching reading lies in the teacher reading the books to the children first. A lot of teachers may be taken aback by this suggestion. Some teachers might find themselves prevented from following it by a shortage of good reading books. Most simply have not realized the advantages that flow from reading books to children that children are expected to read as part of a strategy of always working from the known to the unknown. First of all, children have an excellent memory for stories that have been read to them. Once they have the context to guide them they can predict unknown words so much more easily. They can quickly spot the names of characters, places, and so on. Any illustrations make immediate sense and provide further clues as to what is happening in the text. It has been estimated that reading a book first to a child brings down its readability level by as much as two years. A book is not spoiled for a child when he knows what happens next. He wants to relive the pleasure he got from hearing the story, probably many times over, leading to the further pleasures of familiarity and mastery of the words. Upon this achievement the child is level with the teacher. He has read the book the teacher read and so he does not labour under the notion that there are teacher's books and children's books, or hard books and easy books. There are only books that you have read and books that you haven't read yet. Of course I do not suggest for one moment that the teacher should limit her reading aloud to only those books the children can read too.

How books catch on

Reading books to children performs the simple task of introducing good choices of reading. How can beginning readers select an appropriate and enjoyable book? They are either forced to read certain books, such as a reading scheme book, or, if they are given freedom, they can only go by the cover and the illustrations. Adults, who have built up a lifetime's experience of choosing books, often fail to realize the helplessness of a beginner: we choose books as a result of recommendations and review, in order to follow a favourite author, or a certain style or subject, and by quickly sampling the text or reading the blurb. In spite of all the personal skill that develops, it is striking that most bestsellers these days are 'spin offs' from television programmes.

Television seems to play the role of introducing adults to new and old writers that the teacher plays with her children. The book the teacher reads becomes the instant favourite. There is a queue to read it. It is surely desirable to associate reading with this kind of eager enthusiasm rather than to ask a child to make his way alone through an unfamiliar text. For a few, the task may be intellectually stimulating but for many, it is a chore which keeps them dependent on the teacher. A child who is reading familiar material has been helped towards independence, taking up less of the teacher's time with unknown words. Above all, he is choosing to read alone for pleasure. He is making far more progress than he possibly could if restricted to reading practice with his teacher.

Books that really catch on are read not once but many times over. Excitement and humour seem to bear endless repetition for children. Just as little children love to hear their favourite stories over and over again (and the younger they are the more undeviatingly word perfect they expect you to be), so older children love to reread their favourite books. In rereading, the child is not just marking time: he is getting repetition in a natural and pleasant way, not associated with forced texts and drills. He is developing both fluency and speed. He is developing those skills we cannot teach him, the skills of the accomplished adult reader.

Rereading can be fun

When I first began teaching, the idea of asking a child to read his book again filled me with the kind of dismay that usually showed on the child's face. Was it any wonder, when the book was a thick volume from a stodgy, old-fashioned reading scheme, such as 'Janet and John' or 'Happy Ventures'? It was not just the tedium of the text but the apparent demotion and the waste of many months of work. Children were clearly demoralized. With different books, different organization and different psychology I have changed my mind about rereading. Not only do I take advantage of the children's natural desire to reread favourite books but I encourage children to reread their primers and I make certain that slower children read them several times over. Children weigh their pleasure in rereading to the teacher against their acute awareness of their own progress through a reading scheme, however well this is disguised by colour coding and 'individualizing'. The skill of the teacher lies in making rereading appear desirable. She would not say, 'Oh dear you'll have to read that again' which, however sympathetically expressed, would be immediately perceived as a sign of failure. She would say something along the lines of, 'Oh I do like that book. Let's read it again tomorrow, or, 'Show your Mummy how well you read that book.'

The best motivation of all is one of those exceptionally good books that I call 'winners', which are so good that I do not even have to suggest rereading. So I have come to the conclusion that it is more important to have a careful selection of such books with magic appeal than a lot of more mediocre books. All of this shows just how vital it is for the teacher to become a skilled observer of children's reading habits and tastes. After all, teachers select and purchase all the books for classroom use and it takes a bit of swallowing to accept that we have much to learn from children. The only way for an inexperienced teacher is to make the best possible selection of books, to read them to the children, to weigh their responses, and then to make careful notes of which become 'hits' and which 'misses', and with which children.

Excuse me, what would be suitable for a six-year-old?

This apparently simple and humble procedure is not followed as often as it might be and the evidence is often to be seen in class libraries in the form of accusingly pristine rows of teacher–orientated books. In a way the problem is more acute at home. In the classroom a certain amount of wastage can be tolerated because few books are not used at all and the best are used by everybody. The wrong choice in the home is a total waste, and unfortunately children are vulnerable to well-intentioned but inappropriate picking by relatives and friends. One overhears them in a bookshop asking, 'What would be suitable for a six-year-old?' A canny parent will find out which are the favourite books of the age group and make sure that aunts and uncles are subtly aware of them. Choosing books for children is such an important – and such a pleasant – job that I have felt it worth going into detail about it in later pages.

Uneventful consolidation

There is a short time when all children are so proud of their new-found skill that they will read and reread. That happens when they master their first reading book. Unfortunately, early enthusiasm for new-found skills does not last. The thrill of riding a bike without falling off, playing a tune on the piano, swimming across the pool, is always followed by a period of uneventful consolidation. In reading this takes the form of a long slow build-up of vocabulary and experience of words and meanings in many different contexts. I would no more expect children to become fluent readers away from books than I would expect them to become proficient swimmers away from water, or expert pianists away from the piano. Of course a swimmer can build his muscles, or learn the technique of strokes on dry land, and a pianist can learn musical theory. These are important but incidental skills which at a pinch could be left out without affecting competence. I have stressed there is only a limited amount of precious time for one teacher to teach many children to read. Insistence upon separate teaching of skills will reduce even further the time available and lead the teacher to neglect the essential task of hearing reading. Those people, both teachers and educationists, who talk about the reading 'problem' and see its solution in providing the child with a battery of skills and 'sub-skills' may consider hearing reading unnecessary. At worst, they will say it is a waste of time.

I am afraid that hearing reading in itself is a humble activity. Children reading in flat halting voices the non-adventures of Peter and Jane for the umpteenth time can send the teacher to sleep. Yet for the child it may be the first time, and the most bored teacher must show enthusiasm and delight. This is the most important expression of the teacher's skill. Of course, the teacher will take part by correcting errors and supplying new words, but the general attitude should be less active intervention, more patient guidance. A good teacher will give the child a chance to correct his own mistakes and predict his own new words. If children are reading fluently and for meaning, the odds are that by the time they get to the end of the phrase or sentence they will spot their own error. The teacher has to develop the art of relaxed and observant listening and must not feel that she has to 'teach at' the pupil all of the time. Sometimes teaching gets in the way of learning.

The way to silent reading

A typical skill of fluent reading that the reader must learn himself (one never mentioned in the usual panoply of skills) is reading ahead of his voice to anticipate the meaning of the phrase or sentence. This form of learning is by its nature bound to lead to apparently careless mistakes. To show how teacher intervention can hinder learning, let me give you two, admittedly extreme, examples of interference by a conscientious teacher. One day I saw Kevin reading, with his teacher covering up the words ahead of the one he was reading because, she said, he looked ahead and they would distract him. Another time I noticed Philip, an advanced reader, resignedly pointing to each word in his book as he read. This was slowing him down to the point where he was losing the thread of a quite sizable story. 'Why are you pointing with your finger?' I asked him. 'Because my teacher says I must, so I don't make mistakes.' Of course fluent readers read so fast that they make a lot of trivial mistakes. The most accomplished newsreader will make an occasional mistake. We sympathize, but we do not think that means he does not know what he is reading. We must encourage fast reading with its consequent mistakes because this is the only way towards silent reading.

There is a sort of sound barrier in reverse. Once the 'silence barrier' has been passed the reader can speed up his reading considerably because he is no longer slowed down by 'vocalizing.' Obviously the ability to read silently is a tremendous step in someone's education and I can think of fewer handicaps than not being able to do so. Yet silent reading comes naturally. It would be pointless for a teacher to say to a child 'Now you are ready to read silently'. The skill of silent reading is yet another skill not mentioned in the official literature. There are no prescriptions, exercises or drills towards the attainment of silent reading. It comes from reading. No teacher can make a child into a good silent reader any more than a gardener can make a carrot. But the gardener can do everything in his power to produce the right conditions in which carrots can thrive. The reading teacher's task is to develop the conditions in which reading can take place at the speed of thought. As one child put it to me, 'I'm reading it in my mind.'

Professional attitudes

There is no mystique about teaching reading. The teacher's role is to develop a child's latent ability to read. She can only go about this by providing texts with controlled vocabulary that suit his needs; time and patience to hear him read; constant encouragement and feedback; tactful help with mistakes; an introduction to books and the time to read them alone. For many teachers this is a satisfying, rewarding and demanding task which develops their professional skill and experience. Others feel there must be more to it than sitting listening to kids read and choosing a few books – anyone can do that. The more extreme of them are flattered by the idea that they are transmitting elaborate skills (and subskills) when they teach reading.

All teachers have a right to feel threatened if it seems their job has been reduced to something so simple that it could be done by any parent. For a mixture of professional, political and technical reasons there has been great hostility to parents, classroom helpers and any other lay helpers getting involved in teaching children to read. But if simply hearing children read is the greatest stimulus to reading progress, why shouldn't they? The answer is that they should, and the teacher must not feel that her role is diminished. Indeed her role could be greatly enhanced if she was able to delegate some of the more routine and time-consuming jobs. I envisage helpers and parents listening to individual children read under the teacher's guidance and control. If there were such a team effort the teacher would clearly be the leader and technical expert responsible for planning and organization, choice of material and methods, decisions about individual children's progress and problems, and assessment of results – much as a doctor having prescribed the treatment leaves juniors and nurses to administer it. The doctor makes the decisions about whether doses should be increased or reduced, the nurses carry out his instructions. The doctor would never waste his valuable expert time in washing the patient and putting him to bed but he might well be prepared to spend a lot of time sitting on the patient's bed listening to him chat. We primary teachers spend a lot of time wiping noses, changing wet clothes, mopping the floor, and doing other unskilled tasks. As a result of this we waste precious time that we could spend in actual teaching and in getting to know our children as individuals.

The skills needed to teach reading

Of all the teacher's tasks, reading is the one that takes the most time and attention. But how much actual skill does it require? I have admitted that anyone can hear a child read but have said that ideally it would be done under the guidance of the teacher. The teacher's special skills lie in planning and organization, observation, and knowledge of the tools of the trade. I would enumerate them as follows:

1) putting reading into the context of general class management
2) making effective use of available resources for reading and where necessary creating new ones
3) planning a flexible reading programme
4) developing a wide knowledge of reading books and materials
5) becoming familiar with the practical psychology of small children and especially their response to praise and encouragement (i.e., motivation)
6) making decisions about when the child is ready for the next stage, and when he needs extra practice
7) assessing and recording reading progress
8) deciding what support activities are needed
9) accurately recognizing remedial needs
10) contributing to the reading policy and expertise of the school as a whole.

I insist that the teacher's main role is hearing reading but there are other more active ways in which she can support the learner reader. Some of these are vitally important but incidental to reading and will be discussed in other chapters. They are writing, spelling, dictionary work and story-telling.

Sounds and symbols

Among the skills which I suggested would not in themselves produce reading ability, phonics is a necessary subject to teach the developing reader, whether or not he is taught by the phonic method. The justification lies in the need to build up an effective reading vocabulary. For this, phonics is an extremely valuable tool. The key questions that arise are when children should start to learn phonics, and what the best uses of phonics are. Elizabeth Goodacre has an interesting discussion in her book *Children and Learning to Read* about the mental age at which children appreciate the relationships between sounds and words. She remarks that a mental age of over seven years seems to be the level of development when children can begin to carry out accurate phonic analysis. In any case, children's general analytic ability is rather slow in developing and most children can make a good start at reading before they can handle phonics.

Once children have grasped the relationship between sounds and their symbols they have a source of extra clues to help with their reading and to predict unknown words. The basic equipment for this comprises knowledge of the alphabet, the name of each letter and its possible sounds, and the combinations of letters and their sounds. Armed with this, the beginning reader can tackle unknown words without necessarily having to break them down into all their phonic constituents. For example the initial letter clue is often sufficient. 'The cowboy jumped on his h____.' With the all-important contextual clues and the initial letter there is no need to analyze the word phonically. Of course this leads to occasional mistakes, but these are usually self-correcting. We have already discovered that even beginning readers seldom read letter by letter. Their eyes may jump to some familiar grouping. Teachers' evidence for this is the silly mistakes children make, such

as the classic confusion of 'kitten' and 'little' in the first
books of the 'Janet and John' scheme. They are obviously
identifying the word by the grouping of 'itt'. This tendency can be turned to good account by teaching children
families of words which allow them to read unknown
words by analogy. Some confident readers become so
skilled at this they can read a difficult passage or sail
through a reading test without much of a clue as to the
meaning of what they are reading. This facility could be
too much of a good thing if it divorced 'reading' (for
sounds) from 'comprehension' (of meaning). But of course
it only becomes critical in the artificial conditions of a word
recognition type of reading test.

Such phonic activity, of course, shades over into spelling
and writing but is not to be relied upon exclusively. Purely
phonic spelling is disastrous. As with any language skill,
experience and repeated exposure to words count for far
more than the prior learning of rules. The more a child
reads the more likely he is to see whether he has spelled a
word correctly. Only when you have written a word can
you see whether you have spelled it correctly. My general
conclusion is that excessive dependence by the teacher on
phonics could get in the way of the learning of reading,
where the visual aspects must take precedence.

The rudiments of phonetics

It is appropriate at this point to mention phonetics, with
which phonics is sometimes confused. Phonetics is the
scientific study of the sounds of language. Phonics is a
teaching technique which draws on the rather imperfect
correspondence between the signs and sounds of English.
All children should have some incidental knowledge of
how language works, and I recommend teaching children
the rudiments of phonetics. The only apparatus needed is a
mirror, then children can see and feel for themselves the

different positions of their lips, teeth and tongue in sounding different letters. This extra scientific understanding can make all the difference to a phonic problem. The other day I was looking at a 'Laugh and Learn' reading book with six-year-old Delroy. He was having difficulty with a phonics page of pictures of things beginning with 'g'. 'Delroy,' I asked, 'What sound first comes out of your mouth when you say the word ghost?'

'Boo!'

The last word on phonics.

'Teaching reading from behind'

Because children learn to read at different rates the gap between the most and the least able becomes progressively wider. This creates something of a teaching problem. Ideally a teacher should be able to give each child an individual reading programme, but if this does not prove possible a flexible approach should be used with the available materials. Teachers have to be on their guard against a number of dangers. When, as often happens, they group children by ability, they have to be alert for the reader who becomes capable of forging ahead and gets frustrated when held back. There is a rather more subtle problem with the slower learners of such a group when teachers, anxious for steady progress, give them books that are slightly too hard.

Every teacher of reading is familiar with the child who finds his reading difficult, hesitates too much, and becomes restless and bored. A teacher must straightaway give that child an easier book to restore his confidence. I go along with Beverley Randall, the New Zealand author of many successful reading books, who says, 'You cannot give children too many easy books.' She calls it 'teaching reading from behind'.

However, a teacher has to be on her guard not to give a

slow reader material that suits his level of ability but which he regards as babyish. Normal reading schemes are geared to the average age progression. A tough eight-year-old boy who has struggled to the third book of the 'Janet and John' reading scheme is liable to feel insulted at having to read about Teddy bears, dolls and toy trains. Even if he is not, he will be conscious that the books he is reading were long ago discarded by most of his classmates. This is an argument for the special reading schemes that have been designed for the late starter, and for providing individual reading books that are simple but at a more suitable emotional level. It is often a difficult job deciding what the priorities are, especially as books get more and more expensive.

Difficulties boys have with reading

I mentioned a tough eight-year-old boy deliberately. It happens that the majority of late starters and slow readers are boys. Girls usually make an earlier start to reading and draw ahead of boys. I do not think this is to do with any difference in intelligence and ability. It reflects boys' more active temperament. It is no coincidence that in reported cases of 'dyslexia', boys outnumber girls by five to one. As an activity reading is much less popular with boys who prefer to play and make things. They are less likely to choose to read in their leisure time and therefore often do not realize their potential without a lot of very careful work by the teacher. She has to capture and maintain their interest with more stimulating and exciting books than girls seem to require. Fewer boys use the public library on their own initiative. They tend to favour non-fiction and books about football, indicating perhaps that they give books less intrinsic value.

I realize that even the mention of this observable difference in attitude and taste between the sexes will upset the people who worry about 'sex role stereotyping' in children's literature. They seem however to be more concerned about the unconscious demeaning of girls in children's books. My concern is a very practical one, that a lot of reading books fail to give boys the interest and excitement that will allow reading to compete with other things. As the majority of primary school teachers are women there is a risk that boys' interests are not fully appreciated, especially when it has become démodé to think in terms of biological differences.

How parents can help with reading

Parents of very active boys who are reluctant readers can do a lot to help. They should make a special effort to follow the advice that I would give in any case to all parents: to co-operate with the school and to encourage their children. The way to keep up the reading momentum is to get the right kind of books to read to the children in an entertaining and enthusiastic way, and of course to listen to children read as often as possible. These days parents may feel it is difficult to find either the money or the time. However, they will require not more than fifteen or twenty minutes a day and a short trip to the library once a fortnight. Parents do need some expertise in helping their children to select books. Teachers have greater opportunities to observe children's tastes. On the other hand, parents have the chance to experiment with books that might get submerged in the classroom where the deciding factor is the attention of a group audience. The measure of success of a book is the amount of happy interest the child shows. Once a child becomes bored and restless, discard the book. It is probably a wrong choice. Parents ought never to be short of advice on the choice of books. Teachers and local librarians are always glad to help. There are children's book clubs and magazines for parents. I have drawn together my own recommendations and some useful references at the end of the book.

In the early stages of learning to read there will be a wide gap between the kind of book the child enjoys listening to and the very limited material that he is able to read. Parents should consult the teacher on the choice of beginning books and, if possible, borrow them from the school, because there is not a great selection of very simple books for sale and in public libraries. Children should never be asked to read books which are beyond them. On the other hand, parents should always have the patience to listen to the umpteenth rereading of an old favourite. Apart from the pleasure the child is getting, he is reinforcing and revising his reading skill, and practising to become a fluent reader.

All children like a period of quiet attention and appreciation from their parents and what could be better than a read and a cuddle. If hearing children read and reading to them is a happy time, children will want to do it. If it is surrounded by nagging and criticism, the child will avoid it. It could even do harm and slow down a child's reading progress. For this reason some teachers are unenthusiastic about the idea of parental involvement in the teaching of reading, but if a teacher of a class of thirty children was able to rely on each child getting fifteen minutes enjoyable reading practice every day with Mummy or Daddy it would be a teaching bonus equivalent to two extra school days a week. Daily reading practice would be of special value during the school holidays, when children tend to slip back a bit.

7 Writing and Spelling

Early techniques

The best way to start writing is to encourage children to paint, draw and crayon. The skills and techniques they develop are exactly those that apply to writing, for example, holding and wielding a pencil in order to make satisfying marks on paper where you want them, and going on to develop the co-ordination of hand and eye, and control of the fingers, to make these marks more and more precise and detailed. The more a child draws the easier he will find the formation of letters and words. Nowadays it is the usual practice for a child to learn to form letters by tracing captions to his drawings. The teacher writes in large well-spaced script a simple caption dictated by the child. Occasionally the child goes into too much detail about his picture and the caption needs to be edited. If the teacher uses the child's own words, it will be more interesting to him and he will be able to read it back more easily.

The word most interesting to a child is his name. Teachers make use of this by giving each child his name card to trace. Frequently it is the first word a child learns to read and write. He can also learn to recognize it by finding his name card among a pile of others, matching it to his name on his coat peg, his drawer or his book, and modelling the letters in plasticine.

Children go on from tracing to copying – for example, writing a caption underneath the teacher's writing instead of tracing over it. Gradually, as their control of the pencil improves, the size of the teacher's letters and her spacing can be reduced. It will be seen then that children learn to write by using whole words and sentences rather than by learning to make individual letters and combining them into two- and three-letter words. They are learning in a purposeful way and learning the words as they need them. This was not always the case. Children used to learn writing in a 'phonic' way. It is odd that no such controversy surrounds the teaching of writing as it does reading. There is, however, plenty of argument about the teaching of handwriting and spelling.

Handwriting

Children's first writing of words and sentences usually employs a simple printed script following the teacher's model. Whatever form handwriting takes it must involve the joining of such letters. One imagines that if handwriting were not taught, the cursive form of printing would evolve as children needed to write more quickly and efficiently.

The majority of teachers show children the most economical formation of letters. Left to their own devices children have a hundred and one ways of shaping their letters. I suspect that only a small number of teachers then go on to teach a particular style of script. To my mind, while conscious of my own scrawl, it hardly matters. Most people's handwriting 'degenerates' into their own individual style, which is an expression of their personality both in its general appearance, and, if we are to go along with graphologists, in the minute details of letter formation. This individualism expresses itself at a very early age as soon as children can string a few words together. What is remarkable is that most handwriting is legible and all hand-writing is decipherable. We are back to the whole area of 'distinctive features'. However badly formed the

letters, they belong to families of shapes and it is soon
evident what they definitely are not, what they probably
are, and then what they mean. Teachers' argument for
delaying the introduction of a cursive script is that lower-
case printed letters resemble the print in reading books.
Whatever their feelings about handwriting neither teachers nor parents should accept untidy presentation, making
due allowance for children's different ability to handle
writing materials. There is also the problem of left-hand-
edness where, as is well known, the action of writing risks
smudging what has just been written. My emphasis is on
overall presentation rather than elegance of handwriting
which is attained by few. The reason is somewhat defensive. Some parents set enormous store by written work.
They mean by this its neat appearance rather than its
content. Every teacher can testify that on open days such
parents will tour classrooms comparing the neatness of
handwriting without any regard for the content and style
of stories, drawings and so on.

Why writing is harder than reading

Writing and reading, although twin aspects of language,
soon begin to diverge for a very simple reason. Writing is
more difficult than reading. Recognition is easier than
recall. You cannot write that which you cannot read.
Anyone who has a smattering of a foreign language knows
that it is far easier to translate from it than to translate into
it. The man in the schoolboy joke who claims in his job
interview that he can write but can't read is another
illustration of this phenomenon. When his half-baked
ability is put to the test he covers the page with marks. Asks
what it says he replies, 'I dunno. I told you I can't read.'
Silly, but it draws attention to what even teachers may fail
to appreciate – the idea that children can be taught to read
by means of their writing books.

You can doubtless predict that my philosophy of learning to write is that you get better the more you do of it. But if teachers insist that reading and writing remain in parallel they slow down both processes. This may represent an undue constraint on the amazingly quick but relatively limited short-term memory in the brain. In any case a child's ability to read will forge ahead of his ability to write. Indeed, it must do so if he is to construct his own sentences rather than copy the teacher's writing. Learning to write will certainly reinforce learning to read in the early stages. When a child copies a word, he has to take a very close look at the way it is made up. So, thinking back to the use of flash cards, the written detail of the word supports the memory of the whole form.

I have noticed that some children with poor manual control, who are therefore unhappy when writing, can become fast and fluent readers. One little boy, with a darting eager manner and a nervous shaky hand, completely refused to write during his first two infant years and did badly on so-called reading readiness diagnostic tests that required him to use a pencil. In the meantime, however, his reading went ahead by leaps and bounds, to the point where his performance on a reading test was well above average. This kind of imbalance between reading and writing is by no means uncommon. A contrasting child, who was quiet and reserved, literally shrank from writing and as a result was held back by his teacher who assumed he was unable to read. Taken over by a new teacher he learnt to read in two weeks and became an avid reader.

Writing readiness

A child ought to have started writing by himself by the time he can draw on a pool of about one hundred words that he can read. If he hasn't, he should be given a push.

The beginning writer has to be given confidence and know-how. Here is how it works. A child will come to the teacher for his caption. The teacher asks, 'What shall we put?' The child, if not in a particularly creative mood, may decide he would like to say 'Here is a house'. The teacher would first of all suggest that 'Here' is a word that he already knows. 'Didn't we write it yesterday? Why don't you look at what you said about your last drawing?' 'Is' and 'a' are simple words which he should be able to manage. What about 'house'? The teacher might suggest that he go over to the Wendy House and find the word 'house' on the notice that says 'Four children may play in the Wendy House'. Plenty of such references and reminders can be provided for the beginning writer. Some words will come from flash cards, some from wall captions, as the teacher will probably find it helpful to have lists of commonly used words on the wall. Although this is still copying rather than writing, what counts is the independence it creates and the practice at finding and recognizing words for oneself, the beginning of dictionary skills. Very soon the human law of least effort starts to apply. When a child has had to get up, find and copy a word several times he will begin to find it more convenient to use his memory. He will also see the time and effort he can save by maintaining a personal dictionary.

Dictionaries

When a child wants to know how to spell a word he finds the appropriate initial letter in his personal dictionary for the teacher to write the word. Two good commercial versions of personal dictionaries are available from Philip & Tracey and from Longman. The teacher can easily convert a plain notebook into a dictionary with a letter and perhaps a little key drawing at the top of each page. Ideally, a letter-indexed notebook along the lines of a telephone address book would be handiest, and I am surprised that no one has produced such a thing.

The next stage is the picture dictionary, of which there are a number of excellent versions. The major drawback of picture dictionaries is the limit to what can be illustrated. By the very design the compiler has to make a small selection among the many objects he could usefully show, but many necessary words in the beginner's vocabulary do not lend themselves to illustration at all, words such as 'about', 'after', 'because', 'wants', 'said', 'their/there', 'very', 'were', 'when', 'you' which are frequently used words and difficult to spell. In spite of this limitation, picture dictionaries can bridge the gap between the home-made word book and the dictionary proper. Even an abridged adult dictionary is too daunting for a child, who is in any case not concerned with definitions at this stage. On that account the best first dictionary for young writers is the alphabetical spelling list, published in three literally 'handy' sections by Wheaton, together with a teacher's manual. This list originated in New Zealand and was based upon a study of children's vocabulary and the frequency of word use, drawing on extensive research by the Board of Education of the City of New York. Only very slight alterations had to be made to take care of English cultural differences.

Good elementary dictionaries for use in primary school are the Chambers series *Dictionaries One to Four,* and Black's *First Writing Dictionary.* The use of basic dictionaries does not make the child completely independent of the teacher in his search for spelling. He can only use a dictionary successfully once his reading ability allows him to recognize the word he seeks on a list, which in a way is contradictory. The child also needs to develop the rather advanced skill of looking at the second and third letters in a word alphabetically. After all this, there will be the inevitable frustration of discovering that many of the words he needs are not in the abridged dictionary, or that he is unable to find words because he is mispronouncing them, for example 'free' as in the cockney 'one, two, free'.

Words your children use

Schools using 'Breakthrough to Literacy' enjoy the benefit of the ready-made words forming the basis of a built-in dictionary, although it can become unwieldy as the volume of words a child needs increases. Teachers preparing word lists or elementary dictionaries, and planning writing activities, would be well advised to utilize the infant vocabulary survey of *Words Your Children Use*. These lists of words, most used by children at five years, six years and seven years, show the growth of vocabulary and the changing outlook of children during their very rapid development in infant school. They also show that the two most widely used reading schemes are somewhat at odds with the way children actually use language. Although not exactly bed-time reading for teachers, these lists can be dipped into and analysed for two important purposes. The first is to study the structure of our language, whether used by small children or adults, in particular the way a very small number of words act as carriers in the sense that they 'carry along' the main nouns, verbs, adjectives and adverbs, and express recurring relationships and statements. The second purpose is to get insights into the way children's language differs from that of adults and reveals their changing thoughts and preoccupations. For example, 'I' never drops below fourth in these lists but would be much lower in a correspondingly adult list, as we express our egotism in more subtle ways.

The world children write about

These vocabulary lists show that children are at ease with

the past tense, in spite of the impression given by reading schemes that they exist in a perpetual present. The words 'went', 'saw' and 'was' retain a high ranking through the various age groups. Nevertheless the development of a narrative style appears in the greatly increased use of words such as 'then' and 'when' as children get older and in the progress of the word 'and' from number six at the age of five to the prime position by the age of seven. For, as every teacher knows, the word 'and' is children's favourite punctuation device. Perhaps the most telling message of the lists is the way in which children's writing is rooted in the real world which their reading books do not always represent. This is well demonstrated by a comparison of words which appear in *Key Words to Literacy* compiled by W. Murray and J. McNally, the authors of the 'Ladybird' reading scheme, with the first two hundred and fifty words of children's own writing. The difference, of course, is between words children encounter in reading books and those they employ in their own writing. As nouns give the best flavour of language, let us look at those which appear only in the Key Words list. They include 'bag', 'cow', 'cup', 'egg', 'hat', 'hill', 'jam', 'milk' and 'pig'. The corresponding list of words exclusive to children's writing include, 'afternoon', 'aunty', 'birthday', 'brother', 'colour', 'football', 'friend', 'game', 'holiday', 'people', 'rocket', 'television', 'tomorrow' and 'yesterday'. The first thing to notice is that most of the children's words are much longer (and less 'phonic') and, of course, they reflect much more a world of events and relationships.

Although without doubt children's own words are more personal and exciting, there is a price to be paid. A child's world can be a very narrow one. When you have read for the umpteenth time a child's account of how he spends his time on the lines of 'Yesterday I went to my aunty and my brother came and we played football and we had some ice cream and I drew a rocket and after I went home and then I

watched television' and so on, you may long for a simple
story in which a cow met a pig going up a hill. Fortunately
children are not required to read each other's creative
writing.

Occasionally children's writing is striking, either
because of its charm and innocence, or because of amusing
revelations about their home life. The difference between a
pedestrian style and one that comes alive is shown by the
following two stories.

Jacqueline's story

Yesterday I went to a party, and the place where I
went to had a baby, and at the party we had jelly and
ice cream and cakes and the name of the baby is Terry
and the name of the baby's mummy is Susan and the
name of his daddy is John, and the baby has a lot of
toys and he is funny and I read a book and I played
with his toy's. And then I had a drink and then I had
another drink again, and then my sister had a drink
and then I played a game with the baby called Terry
and then I run round, and then we went in a car and
we went off in the car for home.

Maureen's story

Last Sunday I watched T.V. when I pushed the
button on B.B.C. 2 guess what I saw. I saw Church of
God it was great I saw a lady she was jumping up and
down and she had the spirit, then an Indian lady
started to jump and scream all about the place then I
saw a man doing the same funny thing and all of them
started to sing a song. I forget what song it was, the
frightening thing I liked best, was about the spirits

and the man holding a baby in his hands. My uncle Peter was there too he is tall dark and handsome and he is my mums boy friend he goes to work and does not lay in bed any more, sometimes he takes my mum out to have a good time, sometimes he gives me money and I spend it on sweets, I stay by myself when my mum goes out and watch television I am not frightened and sometimes I turn off the light and when I get hungry I take some cream crackers out of the safe and I put butter on my cream crackers and it tasted good when I put some butter on to it and some crumbs fell on the floor and my cat started to eat the little crumbs that fell on the floor.

It is better to write a little about a lot of things

The fact that some children are capable of vivid imagery and skilful story-telling has led to children's writing being generally overrated. It seemed that all you had to do was to free children from copying, dictation and formal composition and you would release a creative urge. Unfortunately creative writing comes no more easily to most children than it does to most adults. Writing is a somewhat tedious chore which you can only become good at by practice. The teacher's skill has to be directed towards making the task as interesting as possible. Even with free writing she has to encourage children to write and guide them as to what to say.

The first sentences a child is asked to write are usually captions to his drawings and models. If he is bursting with something to say the teacher will probably ask him to write his 'news'. In my opinion the writing of children's news is rather overdone. Children do not have exciting things to recount every day and once a child realizes everything has to be written down he may decide to keep his news to himself. The answer is to avoid a routine approach to writing, aiming at short, varied sessions which ring the changes on captions, news, and other forms of writing.

Beginning writers have to cope with the difficult mechanics of forming letters, finding spellings, spacing and punctuating their words, and writing in straight lines, so they cannot be asked to write too much at a time. One sentence is enough. A child can actually be asked to 'say one thing about...' a particular subject. There are endless possibilities with such a simple formula. It can follow a discussion, an event, looking at a picture, and so on, and most children can manage one simple sentence. Once they have got used to thinking what to say, they may themselves want to expand their writing. It is better to ask young children to write a little about a lot of things than a lot about one thing. More will come from asking for statements about 'a car', 'a bus', 'an aeroplane', 'a ship', and so on than asking for a detailed description of any one of these. Discussing the subject with a group of children or the class as a whole will raise more ideas, but, as often as not, the children will play safe in what they choose to write. A discussion about 'my friend' led to a lot of very interesting oral statements, but then the majority of children sat down and wrote 'so- and -so is my friend because he plays with me.' Perhaps the beginning writer prefers a simple statement because he has to keep so many things to the forefront of his conscious mind when he writes.

Everyday uses of writing

There is a wealth of pictures that can be cut out of magazines or looked at in books as an inspiration for writing. Teachers will also provide subjects and story lines. However, there is no point in feeling guilty if somehow powerful creative prose does not ensue. The essential task is to learn the craft of writing. Children will never get a chance fully to exercise their imagination until they have a full grasp of the language. Too much of a concern for fine writing can also lead to a neglect of equally important everyday uses of language for descriptive or instructional purposes. This could include writing a letter to a friend in hospital, writing an invitation to a school event, writing a shopping list or a note to the milkman, writing up the results of a science experiment, writing labels and signs, and so on. For such purposes the simple exercises found on workcards and busy books are useful.

A high-flown and sometimes ideological view of children's writing has led to a disdain of copying. It is essential to learn to copy accurately and in any case some children enjoy copying. As with other learning tasks copying got a bad name when it was a long daily grind, as often as not associated with punishment. While children appreciate the safe and settled aspects of routine, they react very badly to sameness and lack of variety. For children novelty is not just pleasant, it is vital. In spurring them on to write I would use different sizes, shapes and colours of paper, including 'shape' books cut down from conventional exercise books. There could be a 'house' book, a 'ship' book, a 'car' book and so on which children could take turns to write in.

Writing and drawing

Some variety of writing implements will also help to maintain interest: different colours and thicknesses of pencils, ball-point pens, fibre and felt tip pens, etc. I don't think it is wise to ask infants to write with thick crayons, as is sometimes recommended. I imagine this arose as a reaction to making children cramp their early attempts between fine lines and a feeling that, just as their creative spirit would be boldly expressed in paint with fat brushes, their writing would be even more creative with bold crayons and large untrammelled sheets of paper. In practice blunt crayons are very frustrating for young children trying to make letters. Children learn to write best with ordinary size pencils and pens, providing they make an easy mark. I would favour soft pencils such as 'B's or '2B's, and most of the time felt or fibre pens are preferable to ball-points. Although writing and drawing go together, the criteria are different. Generally children need to be encouraged to be expansive and expressive in their drawing and painting. Whereas the making of letters they need fine control and neatness from the start. But once children get to the stage of making their own words, their writing often becomes very small and cramped and they have difficulty laying it out in straight lines on their plain white sheets of paper. Unfortunately lined paper has become frowned upon in infant classrooms, no doubt as a reaction to its previous restrictive use. Even adults need the support of lines when they write, although it is polite to pretend, as with letter writing pads where a lined underlay is supplied, that you do not.

A crisp new writing book

It seems unfortunate that the young writer has yet another thing to worry about, along with deciding what to say, how to spell and form the words, and how to space them. Early stories can sometimes finish up as a disappointing jumble of shaky lines going up and down and crossing over each other. Exercise books are available in a variety of line widths which can be suited to different stages of writing. I would suggest using large sheets of plain paper in the first phase when the child has to copy the teacher's hand, and paper with widely spaced lines when the child is writing on his own. It seems to me as cruel and unnecessary to deprive a child of guide lines as it is to force him to cramp his letters into narrow spaces.

The value of novelty does not cease for older children.

The worst symbol of dreary toil is a thick, grubby, dog-eared exercise book. Fresh learning calls for frequent fresh starts in a crisp new writing book. Most school writing books are too thick but they can be easily split down into several thin ones. Writing books can also be made quickly from a few sheets of paper using a long-armed stapler. Children enjoy doing this for themselves.

Writing is hard work

When children first start writing they require an enormous amount of help from the teacher. The first writing they produce will have needed a discussion with the teacher in order to decide what to say, the teacher writing it down for them slowly and carefully, and listening to them read it back. When the teacher's writing has been copied, she will need to see it and probably hear it read again. This has to be a painstaking process, and the short cut of simply getting a child to trace over something the teacher has written has to be avoided. A child learns as much about writing from discussing the choice of words, observing the teacher writing them, and reading them back, as he does from practising the formation of letters. So in view of the limitations of the teacher's time that I have frequently commented upon, there is no point in getting the child to write more than the teacher can cope with. It is pointless to have all the class engaged in writing at the same time. As usual, the best method is to have one or two small groups writing while the rest of the class are engaged in some less demanding activity. Writing is hard work but, too often in the primary classroom, hard work is writing. Children sitting down writing is the clearest evidence that work is being done and that order and discipline are being applied. In my observation, when writing is treated as a collective daily routine much less of value emerges. Children will tend to stay within their limits and fill out the time drawing the same old pictures with the same old captions, and boring themselves with their 'news'. The only thing they learn is how to make a little effort go a long way.

How do you spell 'fission'?

When the majority of the children in a class become able to construct their own sentences they will still need just as much help from the teacher. They will come to her frequently for spellings. I regard it as a bad sign to see in a classroom a long and impatient queue of children waiting for spellings. It is unproductive and frustrating all round – yet another reason for keeping specific activities to one group at a time. Even with the use of wall cards, word lists and dictionaries, children will still need to ask the teacher for many spellings. If she has to cope with too many at a time she will feel she is turning into a spelling robot, but if the rate of spellings is kept under control and the teacher has a positive attitude, a great deal more can be learned. I broadened my knowledge when a small boy asked me would I please write the word 'fission' in his word book. 'Fission?' I asked. Was he, I wondered, writing a science fiction epic? Alas, no, he was describing the 'fish 'n' that goes with chips.

The most valuable thing a teacher can do when supplying a word is to spell it aloud letter by letter as she writes it down, and then to get the child to spell it out too. With enough practice at this she will soon only have to give spellings aloud.

When the child has finished his writing he should be asked to read it aloud to his teacher. This way he will spot some of his own mistakes. Later the teacher will expect him to have done this before showing her the work. This is the most important form of correction. Children do catch a lot of their own mistakes in time.

Dealing with mistakes

When a child has written his first words it would be a great mistake to correct any aspect of his writing, spelling or layout. His first efforts, whatever their appearance, must receive fulsome praise and encouragement. Only later should the teacher gently point out lack of spacing, poor handwriting and misspelt words. The mildest criticism or correction of his very first efforts at writing may make a child feel demoralized. It is hard for adults to appreciate just how many skills a child has to combine when beginning to write, such as deciding what to put, holding the words and phrases in his mind while he looks up many of the spellings, and forming the letters correctly. Is it any wonder that he overlooks spacing and that his words run into each other? Children have to be encouraged because only by writing copiously will they learn to write efficiently. Writing has to become almost automatic. Good spellers do not hesitate. It is only when we as adults linger over a word that we become uncertain of the spelling.

Once a child has been writing by himself for a few weeks he should be gently guided towards well-formed, well-spaced and correctly spelled work. The teacher should not attempt to correct all the mistakes in a piece, but just select a few of the most important ones to point out to the child immediately. There is no benefit whatsoever in marking written work in the child's absence. Marking should be done only in the child's presence while the work is fresh in his mind, so that the teacher can discuss his errors with him.

One of the most dramatic errors is 'mirror writing' which is most often done by left-handed children. It seems to betoken serious consequences but in my experience it usually corrects itself without lasting harm. The more serious disadvantage of left-handed children is that their writing hand covers up the letters they have just formed, but there is not much we can do about that. Grown-ups who would like sympathetically to recapture some of the difficulty of learning to write, might try writing a few words with their wrong hand.

Some children annoy their teachers unduly by writing in capitals or a mixture of capitals and lower case. This is usually because they are being helped at home. It hardly seems to matter, as they need to know both forms sooner or later. Once they have gained some competence at spelling they can be asked to rewrite their upper case work in lower case.

Punctuation

Until a child has read enough to become familiar with punctuation marks, it is difficult to explain their necessity. In the early stages they are best taught as interesting conventions. Few children have difficulty in learning to separate words in their writing, although there is no such clear punctuation in spoken language. Otherwise early writing reflects the shapelessness of speech. Even the most articulate speaker will punctuate with 'ers' and 'ums' and leave his sentences unfinished. Perhaps the best starting point for teaching punctuation is to read back his writing to a beginner and show that, although he has said a lot of interesting things, they have all come out in a breathless fashion, usually strung together with 'ands'.

The first convention to insist upon is a stop. After saying one thing you make a mark that says stop. When you go on to say the next you use a capital letter to begin your next sentence. The idea of pauses for breath can be extended to commas. The corresponding marks can be pointed out in the child's reading book as instructions to stop, pause and start again 'in a new voice'. Other punctuation marks can be best learned in a rhetorical way. The teacher can act out with dramatic inflection the change of voice that the punctuation marks produce.

Learning to spell

Spelling is an emotive area of education and we tend to judge people's intelligence by their ability to spell. This is unfortunate because accurate spelling is far more difficult to learn than reading. In the last century or so we have made life more difficult for ourselves by insisting on standardized spellings which no longer reflect regional and social differences of speech. It is no longer enough to be intelligible, you must be correct. In English the most commonly used words are mostly those of which the spoken and written versions have diverged the most. Presumably all the words that end in 'ough', for example 'cough', 'bough', 'enough', 'though', 'through', were once pronounced in a similar fashion. Even if English were not so irregular, spelling would be harder than reading because of the fact that recall of a word, i.e., reconstructing it letter by letter from our memory, is harder than recognition, i.e., seeing what the word looks like and what it means as a whole.

Spelling caught or taught?

Margaret Peters in her book *Success in Spelling* illustrated this difference with an experiment involving the word 'saucer'. Less than half of a sample of 967 ten-year-olds could spell the word correctly; 505 of them offered between them 209 alternative spellings and yet, according to the norms of the Schonell Graded Word Reading Test, seventy-one per cent would have been able to read the word 'saucer' correctly at the age of eight. As Margaret Peters says, 'Reading is from the unknown via the context to the known, spelling is from the known to the unknown.' Another recommended book about spelling by Margaret Peters, *Spelling Caught or Taught* argues that spelling is 'caught' by certain favoured children but that the majority of less favoured children need to be 'taught'.

However, if we were to rely on our knowledge of English sounds ten to thirty per cent of words would be quite arbitrarily spelled. The greater part of our spelling is learned incidentally from our reading. From the moment a child learns to write his name, he starts to develop a knowledge, never taught, of the most probable sequences of letters in English words. Almost unconsciously he learns that certain letters usually follow or precede other letters and that other combinations never occur. For instance, an initial 'b' is nearly always followed by a vowel or the consonants 'l' or 'r' and rarely, if ever, by any other consonant. In a similar way an initial 'g' is followed only by a vowel or the consonants 'l' or 'r', and occasionally 'h', 'n', 'w' or 'y'.

Frank Smith gives examples of nonsense words which are easier to say and remember because they follow these rules than those that do not. Margaret Peters describes a similar experiment which showed 'that for random words there was very little difference between good and poor spellers but good spellers were found to recognize nonsense words resembling English much more readily than poor spellers.' She also mentions an international experiment which demonstrated people's skill in handling nonsense words closest to their own language. She concludes that 'the good speller then has learnt the probable sequence of letters in words in his own language and these he has learned visually but the young child without much experience of the look of words has a long way to go before he can unhesitatingly select the correct sequence from the various possible alternative letter sequences.'

Do-it-yourself spelling

As with reading itself, some children have no difficulty in developing the visual skill of spelling. The problem remains of what to do with the poor performers. Part of the answer lies in extra reading practice that gives experience in the look of words. Unfortunately this is not enough to guarantee the hundred per cent accuracy we expect in spelling, as opposed to any other form of language. Spelling has to be taught systematically with rules, mnemonics, and lists of common words to be learned by heart. The rote learning of spelling has been criticized because children are made to learn words which they probably do not need at the time and are likely to forget quickly. The ideal would be to teach spellings of words just as children found the need for them.

This brings us once more to the alphabetical spelling lists compiled by the New Zealand Council for Education Research published here by Wheaton, which I recommended earlier as a dictionary. The words are listed in alphabetical order with a number alongside that indicates to the child whether it should fall within his present working vocabulary. The child looks up a word he cannot spell, i.e., he scans the relevant group of words until he recognizes the one he wants, and if it is at his working level, or an earlier one, he enters it in his own personal learning list. The precise way in which the levels operate is described in an excellent short manual called *Learning to Spell*. The author, Dr G.L. Arvidson claims the chief benefit of the scheme is that it is operated largely by the children themselves, progressing at their own pace, not wasting time learning words they do not need and with a stimulus to move on to a higher level. *Learning to Spell* contains plenty of good advice including encouragement of 'proof reading' by children. The recommended steps are as follows:

> *Seeing.* Look at the word and try to capture a picture of it so that you can see it with your eyes shut.

144   *Reading Success*

Hearing. Say the word carefully several times and listen to yourself and to others until you recognize its sound.

Feeling. See if you can write out the word correctly on paper, without looking at the example you have been learning from.

Look and cover

In my experience the most effective way to learn to spell is the 'look and cover' technique. As Arvidson suggests, you take a mental photograph of a word and then cover it up and try to write it from memory. You then check your spelling and repeat the process until you can always spell the word correctly. This is a better way for a child to learn spelling than simply copying a word directly from a list or dictionary. I also favour written learning with alphabetic spelling, i.e., saying the letters of the word aloud or to oneself, 'aitch' 'oh' 'you' 'ess' 'ee' spells 'house'. This should start as soon as a child knows his letters.

There is no quick and easy route to correct spelling. Although it is greatly helped by reading and writing practice, it requires separate instruction. In a sense it is still a formal subject but ought not on that account to be a strict one. Poor spellers who are discouraged by punishment will avoid writing and stay clear of doubtful words, and thus will be confirmed in their bad spelling.

Does the way you are taught to read influence your ability to spell? It seems as if it ought to be a test of the efficacy of a particular reading method. But the question is seldom put. Margaret Peters carried out modest surveys comparing the spelling of '138 eight-year-olds taught to read by rigorous "look and say" and "phonic" methods' and '230 children taught to read in the medium of i.t.a. and traditional orthography'. There was no difference in the spelling attainment of any of these four groups. However, the type of errors reflected the methods used. For example, phonics – taught children were more likely to go wrong in attempting phonic alternatives. i.t.a. children made similar phonic mistakes, tending to use a minimum of letters, for example 'trafic' for 'traffic', 'herd' for 'heard'. Children relying more on visual references made more 'unclassifiable' errors. Nevertheless the fact remains that the different methods do not affect the general level of spelling attainment.

How parents can help with writing and spelling

The best pre-school preparation for writing is the encouragement of children's drawing. Some children will draw for hours and parents should not stint on paper and coloured pens. Some highly active children never sit still long enough to draw on their own, but all parents should find time to sit down and draw and write with their children. Small children always want to do what adults do and many will have produced their own version of grown-up writing by making rows of squiggly marks all over the paper. A parent can introduce writing by putting a simple caption on the child's picture or showing him how to write his own name. The letters should be in large bold script about 1cm high. Future teachers will be that much happier if the child uses lower-case letters from the start. Children can be shown how to trace over the parent's letters. Tracing paper and tracing books would also be a good investment as tracing would improve the child's control of writing implements. At one extreme there is the child who comes to school unable to hold a pencil, at the other is the child who has been pushed into schooling and already resents such things as writing, copying books and learning in general. Young children should never be taught in an artificial, academic way. It is far better to arouse their natural curiosity and make them want to join in all the interesting things that can be done by writing. You can write a birthday card to the boy next door, address an envelope, jot down a note to the milkman, make up a shopping list, write out a recipe, and so on. When children take part in these activities, saying the words aloud as they write, they can see their enjoyment and value, and gain a motivation to write.

However, we have seen that writing has to be preceded by reading before the child can get much beyond the copying stage. Rather than trying too hard to teach their children to write, parents would make better use of time reading to children, encouraging them to read and making their own reading and picture books. Home-made reading books can be put together by printing simple captions to magazine pictures, pasted in scrap-books. A guaranteed winner is a book about the child himself, built around photographs, drawings and other documentary souvenirs. Variety and freshness are the vital ingredients in any material aimed at young children, so parents should be ready to change the subject of their drawing and picture mounting. They should start a new (thin) book when interest flags.

Unless a child runs short of ideas, the choice of subject should always be his. Once children start school they will probably do sufficient writing in class for parents not to have to press them at home. It is a rare school that does not set great store by writing. There is no reason why parents should not encourage writing if children enjoy it, but probably the more popular activities will be drawing and making scrap-books. Although spelling has a rather grim image at school, it can be great fun at home. There should be at least one good ABC book from the many excellent ones available, so as to ensure a good beginning to learning of letter names and sounds and the alphabet itself. From this ability there will follow many enjoyable word games.

'I-Spy' can be played at any age once children know their letters and is a good standby in waiting rooms or on dull journeys. As children develop their word knowledge Lexicon, Kan – u – Go and Junior Scrabble start to appeal (I have listed other writing and spelling games in the Appendix). Small children can get a lot out of a set of letter bricks. My three-year-old son, sitting one day quietly playing with letter bricks, turned to my husband, and said 'Look, Gordon, I've made your name – G-O-D –.'

8 Measuring Progress

The case for reading tests

In the days when most schools worked their way through a well established scheme of work, probably based on a single reading series, it was apparently easy to assess each pupil's performance and progress. A school using one of the older reading schemes, such as 'Janet and John', 'Happy Ventures', or 'Beacon Readers', would know exactly where a child ought to be in the scheme by a certain age. This rough and ready guide was understood between teachers and between schools. The price of progress seems to have been the breakdown of such a shorthand of reading attainment. The paradox of a freer, more informal and more versatile approach to reading books has been the greater demand for standardized reading tests. Schools were anxious to know if they were doing the right thing; progressive schools, particularly, found that they were subject to the popular mythology of falling standards. The Black Paper writers called for tests at seven as well as at eleven.

Understandably, schools proud of their teaching record, achieved by whatever methods, will be anxious to formulate their achievement. Even when schools do not feel they are under such pressure they will wish to keep inspectors and local authorities informed of their reading prowess. Reading tests will be needed to identify children who would benefit from remedial or special education. Another important justification for reading tests is to guide the transfer of primary children to secondary schools. Some schools will already have used such tests to help put children into streams or sets. Reading tests will be of particular value to the beginning teacher who is eager to find out if she is getting the best out of her children and keeping up with her colleagues. Above all, the justification of reading tests is to allow the head teacher to see whether the school is up to standard and that the children's reading ability and progress compare well with the regional and national norms.

The proper use of test scores

Without such a basis of comparison, it seems to me that a school has no yardstick and cannot evaluate its own performance. There is always a danger that schools could become complacent through ignorance of what is possible. And to reiterate the point, the most progressive and successful school is utterly vulnerable to criticism if it is unable to demonstrate its statistical achievement in the three R's. Thus, while stressing the general importance of reading tests, I would discourage teachers from using them to 'brand' individual children. Reading tests are much more a measurement of the class, the teacher, the school, the method, than of the child. I certainly do not believe that parents should be given individual children's results, since no test is accurate and sensitive enough to do anything more than provide a rough and ready guide for the teacher, in the context of her knowledge and intuition about her children.

Apart from the technical inadequacy of the tests for diagnostic purposes, the results will vary according to the children's personality, mood and approach. The very nature of tests can produce poor results for good but impatient readers who may trip over the verbal hurdles of a reading test. Nervous and shy children may do less well than they ought, while bold and confident children can upset the odds. Every teacher is aware of this aspect of children's performance in artificial test conditions. Therefore, in my belief, the nuances of reading ages and other test scores should remain within the school and preferably with the individual teacher.

What reading ages really mean

The reading age of a child is simply a measure of how he compares with the average score for a given calendar age group, usually at the national level. For example, a child of seven with a reading age of eight has performed as well as the average eight-year-old. Conversely, a child of seven with a reading age of six reflects the average performance of all the six-year-olds. A seven-year-old may undramatically show an average reading age of seven. However, averages, as we are often reminded, conceal more than they reveal. A reading age in itself may not mean a great deal, for several reasons. Firstly, the compilers of all the reading tests are quite open about the statistical error they entail. For example, the manual of the Burt Word Reading test (1974 revision) mentions that, 'when the test has been properly administered an obtained reading age is unlikely to be more than six months in error.' A reading age also has to be interpreted in the light of how long a child has been at school able to read, and of his rate of progress. A seven-year-old child with a reading age of six and a half, who couldn't read three weeks ago, is making explosive progress.

There are two types of reading test, those designed to be given to a single child and those which can be administered to a group. The justification of the latter is the time saved. However, although individual tests are time-consuming, a practised tester, who is familiar with a child's ability and knows where he is in the reading programme, will need to give only the relevant part of a test. The proper application of an individual test requires a child to be isolated and the test to be uninterrupted. This makes it next to impossible for a class teacher to give a series of tests. The head teacher is probably better placed to do that. Simultaneous testing of two or more children obviously cannot involve reading aloud and must depend on some sort of approximation to the 'reading situation'. As beginning readers read aloud for at least a couple of years, perhaps until they are about eight years old, group tests are impractical for such young children.

Group tests

The commonest group tests are of the sentence completion type where the reader has to fill in a missing word, choosing from several similar possibilities and ringing or underlining the right word. One drawback to multiple choice is the chance of right answers by pot luck. For instance, if the right word is to be chosen from groups of four, a random choice will statistically produce twenty-five per cent 'correct' score. In addition, there is a statistical chance of a proportion of children getting all the right answers by chance, without having any clue as to what they are doing. This is yet another instance of the importance of personal interpretation of reading tests. Administered mechanically and taken at their face value, especially by an outsider, they can be very misleading.

The 'cloze procedure' test is now gaining in popularity and although there is a well-known test on the market (the G.A.P. test published by Heinemann), it is easy for teachers to design their own version. All it entails is reproducing a passage and deleting every so many words, then asking the reader to fill in the gaps. Although the cloze procedure is related to sentence completion, it is absolutely necessary for the child to attempt to read the whole passage first to get all the contextual clues. A child who does not read ahead will do badly and a child who has done several tests will gradually improve his performance.

These points raise two interesting questions. The first is familiar to any tester: how far are you testing the ability to do tests? All tests seem to require a certain knack: the practical implication is that children must be taught how to do the test before they can be judged on the results. By definition group tests are formal affairs. Children from a formal classroom, accustomed to silent exercises at their desks, are more likely to take them in their stride than children taught informally, who might be upset by the sudden imposition of examination room conditions. The second question that occurs is how far these tests, that depend entirely for the measurement of reading ability upon guessing from context, penalize children taught by rigidly phonic methods. In phonics teaching the phonically regular word takes precedence over the semantically more probable word and children are discouraged from guessing and taught to 'decode the sound.'

Individual tests

These tests are not strictly speaking, reading tests. They require a child to make linguistic choices and inferences and so call upon his intelligence, general knowledge and self-confidence. However, it does not follow that individual reading tests are any better at reflecting intrinsic reading skill than are group tests. They usually measure only one aspect of reading. One type of test, including possibly the best known, Schonell's Graded Word Reading Test, is based on word recognition. Such tests require the child to read aloud from a list of words arranged in order of difficulty. The limitation of such tests lies in the fact that most reading does not consist of isolated words. Any teacher will be aware that children frequently fail to read words in test lists which they can read quite happily in a piece of prose where they are getting help from the context. A child soon realizes that a test is about getting things right and if he is not a hundred per cent certain of a word, he will hesitate. The very same word in his everyday reading is stripped of doubt by the syntax, and by the impetus of reading unselfconsciously. Often this difference between normal and test performance is a matter of personality and so the teacher can make allowances that an impersonal authority could not.

Another type of test is phonically based, measuring the child's ability to build up three- and four-letter words and other phonic constructions, and using either real words or nonsense words. Once more this is a test of something allied to reading – the ability to sound out phonically regular words from their letters – which does not predict reading competence. Many young children who are fluent readers have great difficulty with this task. The youngest children and the slowest readers find the problem of building up words from sounds beyond them.

I have known children with a reading age of eight, as measured by the Schonell test, who have been unable to blend sounds or even to distinguish sounds within words. Even where children's teaching has emphasized phonics, I can vouch that phonically regular words cause the most difficulty. In many years of giving the Schonell test I notice that among the first group of words

tree little milk egg book
school sit frog playing bun

the word that causes the most trouble is 'sit'. Similarly the phonically regular word 'pet' is a stumbling block on the first page of the Neale test (the Neale Analysis of Reading Ability).

The age bias of tests

The youngest children and those of any age just beginning

to read are not only penalized by group tests, they are inadequately catered for by individual tests. For example, the word recognition tests, which present the child with a graded list of words to read, seems to work on two assumptions. One is that the given word will already be familiar to the child within his sight vocabulary. The second is that the child will be able to synthesize unknown words phonically. As I have mentioned, many young children cannot handle phonics and certainly it is a matter of luck whether test words will be among their tiny beginning vocabulary. The chance is lessened if a single reading scheme is used which highlights words ignored by another scheme. Although a test would cease to have any objective value if it did not represent a standardized measurement, every effort should be made to attune reading tests to the effective vocabularies of young children.

The book *The Words Your Children Use* suggests itself as a useful source. I have compared the first ten words of Schonell's and Burt's reading tests with the hundred most popular words used by five-year-olds. The Burt test comes out of it well, with all ten of its useful looking list, i.e.,

to is up he at

for my sun one of

appearing in the children's list. Among Schonell's first ten words, familiarity with which betokens a reading age of six, only four, 'tree', 'little', 'school' and 'play (ing)', are in the children's top one hundred, thus excluding 'milk', 'egg,' 'book', 'sit', 'frog' and 'bun'.

One set of children is likely to do very well in the Schonell test, those taught to read by the 'Happy Venture' reading scheme. The author of this scheme, F.J. Schonell, includes in it many of the words which appear in his graded test. This hardly seems a scientific thing to do. It would matter less if the Schonell test were not by far the most commonly used test. to date. According to the Bullock

Report, the Schonell Graded Word reading test is used in seventy-two per cent of English primary schools. Most of them are happy to use it in its outdated (1945) form and to overlook a revision by Elizabeth Goodacre.

There is an unfortunate side effect to this. A junior school can justify using word recognition tests to measure reading ability, as they become more applicable when children have built up quite a large vocabulary. Having tested the infant intake, it is not unknown for the junior schools, on the strength of Schonell, scathingly to inform infant school colleagues that their children have poor reading ages. The children may then get unceremoniously shunted back to the beginning of the reading scheme. Both the infant teachers and the new junior children risk being demoralized. There may be less danger of this happening with the Burt reading test (according to Bullock used in a third of English schools), since this venerable Scottish test does not provide norms for a reading age of less than 6.4 years on the grounds of a statistical 'discontinuity' in the relationship between score and reading age for the younger children. The manual explains that at this early stage in pupils' schooling, length of schooling has an effect on level of reading attainment, obscuring the effect of age.

The reading test which I favour as the best of a bad lot is the Neale Analysis of Reading Ability (used in one in six of English schools according to Bullock). It consists of a number of graded passages. Over several years I have correlated the results of Schonell's tests with those of Neale. In my experience, children score significantly lower on Schonell than they do on Neale below a reading age of seven, perhaps as much as a year and a half or two years of reading age difference. Then, between reading ages of seven and nine, the tests become roughly comparable. With reading ages above nine children score more highly on Schonell, sometimes by as much as two years reading age. Yet originally the Neale test, produced in 1958, was designed to correlate with the Schonell test, unchanged since 1945.

The remarkable effects of cultural changes

Perhaps the answer lies in the way language changes over the years, thus altering the validity of reading tests. This would have a bigger effect on word lists, where individual words can become dated, than on contextual tests, where the meaning of even archaic words may still be evident. When the fifty-year-old Burt Word Reading Test was revised and restandardized, the authors found that some words had become easier, and some harder, for children to read. When they re-ordered the words in the test they found that some words had shifted by as many as twenty-eight places. This is extraordinary when one considers that there are only 110 words in the test altogether and that each ten words represents a year of reading age. Thus the word 'glycerine', which has become more difficult to read, had moved twenty-five places down the list, equivalent to two and a half years of reading age. Profound social changes are revealed by the clearly overdue revision of the Burt test. Words that are now easier to read than previously include 'refrigerator', 'emergency' and 'encyclopaedia', all of which have advanced by two and a half years of reading age. Also, scientific words such as 'microscopical' and 'binocular' have moved up by almost a year of reading age. Words which have become more difficult, by anything up to a year and a half, include 'melancholy', 'perambulating', 'labourers', 'fatigue' and 'trudging', which might suggest that children nowadays find it harder to understand hard work and its effects! Similar changes have been reported by other researchers, presumably reflecting both linguistic and environmental changes. Apart from casting rather serious doubts on reading tests which go for long periods without revision, they raise an interesting point about phonics. The Burt test depends, after all, as the manual admits, upon a word-pronouncing capacity. Although the authors are quick to assert this is merely the means to an end, one wonders why phonic analysis is so susceptible to cultural changes. For there are some quite simple words in the Burt test affected by the shifts in reading age. For example, the words 'just' and 'an' have moved up the order of difficulty by eight places although they are phonically regular. Meanwhile the common but phonically irregular words 'some' and 'one' have become easier by more than a year's worth of reading age.

That a test should have been in use in one-third of all primary schools and fifteen per cent of secondary schools, and have been as much as two and a half years 'out', is a serious indictment of the testing system and a pointer for the need for some sort of quality control and advice at government level. After all, our teachers and children are being assessed upon such data, and political capital is being made out of the results.

How dated reading tests disguise progress

The Bullock Report has similar strictures upon the Watts Vernon and the National Survey Form 6 reading tests. Yet the crucial point about these tests and the results from them, is that they formed the basis of the N.F.E.R. report, which seemed to show that reading standards had stopped improving since the middle sixties. This apparently static position was interpreted by the popular press and some unscrupulous politicians as a catastrophic decline. Whatever the truth of the matter, the Bullock committee, apart from dismissing the tests as inadequate measures of reading ability, made what is to me a decisive criticism. Mentioning various dated words in the two tests, they say, 'this is a more telling limitation than might at first sight appear. If with the passage of time even two or three of the items become less familiar the effect upon the test results could be important.' They go on to show that the changes in the reading scores over the years are so slight that contemporary pupils may now be at a considerable disadvantage over certain obsolete words, compared with their predecessors who might actually have seen a 'mannequin' parade and visited a 'haberdashers'. It is also worth mentioning the Bullock Report's concern that the official tests had a 'ceiling effect', which prevented a proper measure of the increase in reading ability of fifteen-year-olds. It appears that for the most able fifteen-year-olds 'reading ability has outstripped the available tests'. The fact that some fifteen year olds can now find their reading tests too easy is perhaps a reassuring antidote to recent panics about reading standards. We have to ask why some people *prefer* to believe reading standards have fallen.

Canaries, horses and frogs

My personal touchstone of cultural effects on reading tests is the word 'canary', which occurs at the nine-year reading age level of Schonell. Presumably this was a completely familiar word in 1945 but then canaries became less fashionable to be replaced by budgies as a household pet, and so most children came to read the word as 'cannery'. However, in the last few years I have noticed that canaries are making a bit of a comeback in council flats where cats and dogs are forbidden, and the word 'canary' is ceasing to be a stumbling block. Yet who could have predicted that milkmen would cease to have horses and that fog would disappear from the centre of London? A sentence in the Neale test reads, 'The milkman's horse had wandered in the fog.' Many children I have tested, who know the word 'horse' (an early 'Ladybird' word), nevertheless read 'the milkman's house'. I was a little puzzled until one boy scornfully told me 'Oh Miss, milkmen don't have horses!'

The children's search for meaning is further hampered by the word 'wandered', which is both a difficult word and a difficult concept, and then by the word 'fog' which is read as 'frog' by children who can perfectly well synthesize three-letter words phonically. Fog has become quite rare in central London but, even though frogs are seldom seen, they are familiar in the classroom through nature study, stories, poems and songs. When meaning is doubtful, children will revert to more familiar concepts in an attempt to make sense and to avoid saying a nonsense word. I will resume this discussion later on in this chapter when we deal with 'miscue analysis'. For what this kind of experience shows is that children's *mistakes* can be extremely revealing and are certainly of great interest to the teacher. This is one of the applications of miscue analysis. But for these discoveries one does not need a formal test.

Blank incomprehension

Cultural bias works most strongly against children with an immigrant background. I recently observed a test of fifty seven-year-olds, mostly of overseas origin, who were taking the N.F.E.R. test A-D, which is a sentence completion and comprehension test with multiple choice answers. I was fascinated by the results for one sentence which read 'The girl was a good dancer because she   ', with the choice of answer

> 1 was so graceful
> 2 was so beautiful
> 3 was very grateful
> 4 had enormous feet.

Ninety per cent of the children who could perfectly well read all the words gave a wrong answer. The girls said it was 'because she was so beautiful'. The boys said it was 'because she had enormous feet'. With unconscious wit and 'sex role stereotyping' they had chosen the only answers available, given their uncertainty about the words 'graceful' and 'grateful'. It would be my contention that a similar group of white children would be much more likely to associate the concept of gracefulness with dancing because of the fashion for Saturday morning ballet lessons. A more direct instance of cultural bias occurred in the same test with the sentence 'Whenever I go on holiday I always try to remember to   to all my friends and relations.' The blank could be filled with one of the following

    1 lend my suitcases   3 pack all my clothes
    2 send postcards   4 travel by train.

A little Bangladeshi girl called me over and asked, 'How can I do this one, I never go on holiday?' Holidays away from home with their attendant customs and rituals are far from being a normal part of the life of immigrant communities.

Tests tell you most about people who design tests. While the limitation of word recognition tests may be obvious, those that try to measure reading *comprehension* are more deceptive. It is the old story of the 'right answer' being confused with the fact that the 'meaning' has been obtained by the reader from a word, a phrase or a whole piece. Those boys and girls who had visions of beautiful or clodhopping dancers had got a lot of 'meaning' from that test item. How well something has been read and how well it has been understood are separate considerations, especially if the reading is set in a different cultural framework. It seems to me that, with a reader who has not fully mastered all the nuances of the language, or who does not understand the conventions of a technical language, the obligation is on the writer to be as clear as possible. (This is a dangerous thing for an author to say. If you do not understand me, it is my fault. Up to a point this is true, although every writer expects a certain amount of effort from the reader.) However, there is no doubt in my mind that if a child can read a passage fluently and yet not understand it, he cannot be faulted. The passage is evidently beyond his general and linguistic knowledge. The purpose of education is to develop the means of understanding and the ability to articulate that understanding. Reading must be the prime tool. With the right kind of teaching and practice we should aim to develop readers who themselves test what they read, who, for example, can expose the mumbo jumbo of an income tax form, the complacency of a self-satisfied piece of jargon, or the ambiguity of a so-called comprehension test.

Comprehensibility

If you separate the mechanics and the meaning of reading and if you further separate the style from the meaning, you will wind up with the absurdities that emerge from a typical comprehension test. First of all I would like you to step up to my desk and read a short passage aloud:

> A robin hopped to my window. I gave her some bread. She made a nest in my garden. Now I look after her little birds.

(While you were reading it, I was marking little boxes. If you made any mispronunciations, substitutions, refusals, additions, omissions or reversals, I ticked the appropriate box. You had 156 possibilities of making an error.) Not letting you see the piece, I now ask you some simple questions. Where was the little boy/girl when the robin hopped up to him/her? The correct answer is 'by the window'. Yet there has been nothing in the piece about a little boy or girl, no mention of a person being by a window. There is only the fact that a robin went up to the window. Similar examples abound:

A surprise parcel arrived for Jane and Peter on Saturday. Peter looked at the strange stamps.

Question: How do you know that the parcel came from another country? Perhaps only foreign stamps were 'strange' when the tests were devised. Now British stamps come in all sorts of strange designs.

Parent foxes share the responsibilities for cub rearing...

Question: Who provides the food for the cubs?

What is striking about all these comprehension questions is that the 'right answer' comes not from an understanding of the text but from making the right inferences from the question. There is no explicit statement about the way the fox cubs are fed, or whether the parcel came from a foreign country, or whether the child was standing by the window. The impression given is that 'comprehension' is a separate entity *under the control of the tester*. The clever child is the one who discovers early on the kind of thing the examiner wants to know.

My conclusion is that comprehension tests measure the *comprehensibility* of a passage for a child and not the child's ability to comprehend. On that account there is no purpose in using them in the teaching of reading. The grasp and the understanding that comprehension tests purport to measure is best assessed by the teacher's continuing observation and judgement.

Diagnostic testing

Once tests leave the area of superficial word recognition

they seem to get into deeper and deeper water. The progress represented by contextual tests seems to lead to new difficulties arising from ambiguity. The newest fashion in tests, so-called 'diagnostic testing', sounds as if it will solve the problem of how to apply the results of tests. I am afraid, however, that diagnostic tests are more impressive in the wish than in the fulfilment. In general, it is very hard to imagine a method of describing a problem that will in itself produce the solution to it. There is always a need for observation, inference, intuition and creativity, all of which a teacher needs and which it is difficult to extract from a battery of tests. As the authors of the best known of these diagnostic tests, Daniels and Diack put it, 'A detailed, qualitative, diagnostic interpretation of the response is now necessary to decide if special remedial treatment is required and what form that remedial treatment should take. Qualitative interpretation is an art which the teacher gains by judiciously blending teaching experience and the scientific understanding of the nature of the skills involved in fluent reading.' They then offer an 'elementary guide to the beginner' in which they are not shy of recommending frequent recourse to their own reading scheme, 'Royal Road Readers'. At best the advice is simply to be methodical, at worst it reminds one of the story of 'Soup from a Stone' in which a beggar persuades a peasant woman to add lots of good ingredients to his magic stone and thereby produce a marvellous soup. Diagnostic testing works wonderfully with a very good, experienced teacher who knows how reading works.

The other off-putting aspect of Daniels and Diacks' prescription is its vaguely pathological flavour. They suggest that you use diagnosis as a doctor would, to seek out a reading disease, a malfunctioning of complex skills (and subskills): you then recommend a dosage of the appropriate remedy. I find this a rather despondent philosophy. The more ambitious a test – and, along with this, the greater its claims to link reading ability to the psychology of the child – the greater the danger of mis-diagnosis. I have long had the practice of taking fluent readers through various reading and pre-reading tests, including the diagnostic ones, and I have ceased to be surprised when I discover fluent readers who ought not to be reading at all. Yet I know there are teachers who take the tests literally and refuse to teach children who are not 'ready'. Perhaps no harm is done; but let me give you a typical example of how misleading a test might be. I gave young Adam test number two of Daniels and Diack Standard Reading Tests: copying abstract figures. Among those the test was recommended for were 'those children whose eye-hand and hand motor control seemed to be impaired.' This in itself would seem to make the result of the test a foregone conclusion and not surprisingly Adam, who was a highly strung, shaky child, made a mess of the task. His drawings were far worse than any of the pathological examples given by Daniels and Diack. Their representative diagnosis would be 'this is a very poor effort... needs a good deal of pre-reading work... little use trying to teach this child to read *until his performance in this task improves*' (my emphasis). At the time the test was given, Adam was six years old with a reading age of nine and was an enthusiastic reader. People might regard this as the exception that proves the rule but, although Adam is a dramatic example, I have tested many ordinarily good readers and found that some of them have done extremely badly in different parts of so-called diagnostic tests.

Miscue analysis

This is a new technique for assessing children's reading aloud by systematically analyzing their mistakes. The preference for the word 'miscue' rather than 'mistake' or 'error' is a recognition of the way in which readers are looking for cues to meaning as they are reading. Some of their mistakes, such as missing out or adding a word here and there, may not affect the meaning. Some other mistakes lose the meaning completely. Miscue analysis was originally developed for research purposes by Kenneth Goodman in the United States. It has been taken up in progressive circles but more conservative teachers have reacted to the apparent endorsement of mistakes. Certainly, by observing children's errors and hesitations, teachers can gain useful insights into the way reading works, and can convince themselves of the reader's search for meaning. However, it must be emphasized that miscue analysis is not a reading test as such but an informal means of assessment. There is a danger in teachers turning themselves into researchers. The teacher's job is to help a child with his mistakes here and now, not to describe them abstractly for some later remedial action.

On the positive side, miscue analysis is to be welcomed as it encourages teachers to let children make mistakes, many of which they will go on to correct themselves. For too long teachers have thought that their role was to jump in and correct each mistake instantly. Children do learn by trial and error and if a phrase or sentence has not made sense they will usually go back and look for their own mistake. As well as encouraging this more patient and productive view of reading, miscue analysis should prevent the teacher from frowning on mistakes that do not interfere with comprehension, for example reading 'has got' for 'has'. On the negative side, miscue analysis could lead to a pre-occupation with classifying reading errors and create a lot of unnecessary paperwork. Endless coding of 'substitutions', 'non-responses', 'insertions', 'omissions', 'pauses', 'repetitions', 'corrections', and other typical errors, could encourage a piecemeal approach to reading and a reliance on mechanistic remedies, such as further exercises and drills, to make up the apparently deficient subskills. We must not lose sight of the fact that children's reading mistakes are most instructive about the style of teaching they are getting and the type of materials they have to cope with. Too many errors may indicate that the text is too difficult, and even if the child manages to wrest some meaning from it, he is not practising the speed and fluency which are essential to good reading. This rather suggests that the teacher's best use of miscue analysis would be to test the suitability and quality of her reading books. The commonest miscues comprise hesitation, non-response and substitutions when faced with unknown words. Too many miscues of this kind may suggest that the vocabulary level is too high or that the context and illustrations are not helpful enough. Another common miscue is an insertion, for example, of a preposition or colloquialism. Such miscues may prompt questions as to whether the style is too stilted and too far from everyday English.

Miscue analysis is something worth knowing about, but is not suitable for assessing an individual child's progress. It is likely to raise more questions than it answers. While hearing children read a passage from the Neale test, I was puzzled by the sudden appearance of a particular miscue. Children kept substituting 'watch' for 'now', which was nonsensical. Then it came to me that all these children had read the first few books of Terry Hall's reading scheme 'Laugh and Learn' where both these words are used prominently. In the time that had gone by, both words had obviously become mixed up in the same mental pigeon hole. Perhaps this kind of association explains other similar 'wild' guesses that children make in their early reading.

Reading tests in perspective

Existing reading tests are limited, archaic, and poor predictors of an individual's reading ability. Some of them may even hide improvements in the reading performance they were supposed to measure. Yet, although teachers might be disposed to think of tests as a necessary evil, they tend to take them on trust. Tests come from on high, they have been designed by experts, they are accompanied by impressive statistical jargon, e.g., 'the application of Kuder-Richardson Formula 20 yields a coefficient of 0.971.' In spite of the jargon, reading tests can only be a rough and ready guide to the reading ability of individuals or groups of children and there is no harm in using any of them with a good pinch of salt at the ready. I have found the Neale test the most useful because it comes closest to actual reading: it is certainly the most suitable for younger children and beginning readers. I use it only as a guide to reading age and do not use the accompanying comprehension tests. In my view comprehension and diagnostic testing are red herrings and lead away from what Bullock calls 'purposeful reading'. I feel that reading tests should only operate as reasonably simple, standardized measures of ability, or as quick administrative indicators; they should be a shorthand between teacher and teacher, between teacher and head teacher, between head and local authorities, and used to test methods, materials and programmes and to assess a school's contribution to local, regional and national performance. There is always a risk that if reading tests are taken too seriously the means might become the end. Something of this is present in the very phrase 'reading standards', which places the emphasis on a minimum achievement, a caucus race which nobody loses but nobody wins either. True reading performance should be measured as a potential and this can only be done at the level of the individual child and the individual teacher.

Unfortunately it is at this level that parents are interested in results. But reading test results, even at the whole school level, are no more than a statistical abstraction. Children with 'correct' reading ages, i.e., children whose reading age and real age correspond, are accidents of arithmetic. I strongly urge parents never to administer a reading test because no single result has any validity. For the same reason the results of school reading tests should never be handed to parents.

Reading records

A teacher should be able to say how well a child reads. Although this will be a matter of over-all judgement, the kind of things she will take into account will be the approximate number and kind of books a child has read, his level of vocabulary, his accuracy and fluency of reading aloud, his speed of reading as a pointer to fully proficient reading, his general attitude to reading, his enjoyment of books and finally his rate of progress. No single reading test, nor indeed any battery of tests, could replicate this kind of rounded judgement. What it all amounts to is that in a school with well trained and experienced teachers, using a well established, imaginative and flexible reading programme, the need for tests will be minimal. The information that people seek from tests will already be available in the form of succinct records for each child.

The ingredients of such records are simple. There should be a brief log of all the reading work done, an indication of where the child is up to within the reading programme, plus any special comments. Relating the record to a total programme emphasizes the positive aim of guiding children to fluent and accomplished reading and also of establishing continuity when teachers change. At the same time, however, a record system must be able to identify exceptional children quickly, usually those who need remedial help, or medical or psychological investigation.

9 Story-telling and Reading

The story-telling tradition

Story-telling is an art as old as fire. Traditional tales and the tradition of creating new tales have come to us over many generations. The same plots, characters and jokes recur in different cultures and languages. 'Careful Hans' turns up in a new disguise as 'Epaminondas'. The naive but happy peasant wends his way through many an adventure. In a book of Italian stories Cinderella becomes Cenerentola, with a magic date tree instead of a pumpkin, and the story of the three little pigs is recast with three little goslings. Many a handsome suitor wins through impossible trials. Once upon a time in any land the best thing to have been was the third son of a poor widow.

For teachers and parents traditional tales are an unlimited heritage but we are also lucky in having so many delightful modern stories. There is always a danger that the story-telling tradition might die away, as its original purpose of home entertainment was long ago supplanted by radio and then television. Apart from such T.V. favourites as *Jackanory*, the main custodians of the story-telling heritage seem to be the schools. Sadly, in some schools story-telling is seen only as a means of filling time during the last half hour between play time and home time. Story-telling is often dispensed with altogether after the infant years, and yet listening to stories is not merely

169

enjoyable, it is a valuable part of a child's linguistic, social and aesthetic education. I believe that if there were more story-telling there would be less need for so-called 'language development programmes'.

Telling and reading

Should stories be told or read aloud? I am often asked this question as if there were a stark choice. There is great value in both telling and reading, and both methods should be used by parents and teachers. The teller can develop a more dramatic style and involve his audience to a greater extent but must depend upon his own phrasing and vocabulary. The teacher reading a story faithful to the language of the author is acquainting her audience with a wider vocabulary and range of style than even the most articulate teller could achieve. It is imperative for the story-reader to have become familiar enough with the text, perhaps to have annotated it, in order to dramatize it effectively while keeping her eyes on the audience. A major advantage of reading aloud is to demonstrate to children the pleasure that can be had from a book. Children will want to read just those books that the teacher reads, hence a canny teacher of reading will read to her children those books that she wants them to read for themselves.

Children seeking to recapture the pleasure of a book they have had read to them, will be better motivated to read, better guided by a familiar context and better able to predict unknown words. In this contextual respect written language is quite different in pattern and form from spoken language. Children who are regularly read to soon come to understand the different conventions. The point is well expressed by Cliff Moon and Bridie Raban the authors of Penguin Books' excellent little guide for teachers, *Penguins in Schools*.

From hearing stories read (as distinct from told)

children acquire a great deal of information.... It includes a whole pattern of intonation, and the clues which it can provide to the meaning of written language. Children who have been read to again and again have heard how adults use phrasing and pitch and pauses to add meaning to the text. They have absorbed without realizing it, the simple but necessary fact that a written story is something one has to interpret. Unless children have experienced some such model of relating a written story to a heard one, they may have real trouble when they go beyond reading schemes in their own reading.

Unless children are read to, they are unlikely to choose to read for pleasure. The Schools Council survey *Children and their Books* mentions that over a third of children do not read books at all after the age of fourteen. The researchers felt that, while there are relatively few 'non-book readers' among ten-year-olds, seeds of later trouble were observable in the primary school, where the emphasis was often on the provision of reference books at the expense of fiction, and where the teacher's guidance in regard to use of fiction was somewhat perfunctory. As they put it, 'The reading of fiction and narrative should not be regarded as peripheral to the real business of growth and learning: for most children it is both essential for the establishment of commitment to reading and important as a means of emotional and intellectual development.'

Another intriguing finding of this survey was that children in junior-with-infant schools were found to read more books than children in junior schools alone. Could this be due to the greater emphasis on story-reading and telling spreading from the infant department? I cannot stress strongly enough the need to introduce books directly to children. Once again the Penguin guide provides valuable advice worth quoting in full.

Merely making the books available in the library doesn't seem to be enough. But a book read on *Jackanory* or serialized or read aloud by the teacher – that book will often become for a time at least, a best seller. Something has happened to make that book accessible to young readers in a new way.

The truth seems to be that a book in unrelentingly solid print, using a written language that may be unfamiliar, telling a story which goes on for one does not know how long or to what effect, is often too demanding a business. But tell children the story (so they know where things are going), give them an idea of the characters (so they know who they are going with); tell them these things out loud (so they hear in the ear some of the rhythms and constructions they will be seeing on the page) then they seem to flock to the shelves.

A book at bedtime

Children are more likely to read books if they have books at home and if their parents read to them. We talk glibly about 'privileged' and 'underprivileged' children or 'advantaged' and 'disadvantaged' children. I have often wondered what privilege or the lack of it was made up of. In my observation it rarely has to do with lack of good food and clothes. Even the social priority schools in which I have taught were full of healthy, well-fed, well-dressed children. Most households have spare money to buy a few luxuries – goods such as televisions, cassette recorders, even cars, which a generation ago would have represented undreamt-of affluence. In our age of material well-being we tend to think of privilege in material terms. It strikes me that perhaps the really privileged child is the one whose parents make the time to read him stories, and take him to the library, and who make sure that some of the available money is used to buy books. Such a privileged child has the opportunity to develop his language to the fullest and his self confidence and imagination grow through the vicarious experience of literature. There must be few greater pleasures of childhood than a bedtime story, or the experience of being read to on a parent's knee. Yet many parents cannot or will not find the time for this engaging duty. What is worse, they lack the repertoire of stories and know-how in choosing books for their 'underprivileged' children.

Hearing for meaning

Reading stories to children presents one of the best ways of increasing their vocabulary and enriching their language. Parents and teachers are apt to speak to children only in words which they think children will understand, thus perhaps undernourishing their language. Books make no such concessions. The child learns as much of his language from reading and hearing books read as he does from listening to adults speaking. A new word will need to be heard many times in many different contexts before it becomes part of a child's repertoire. This was brought home to me recently when I was reading the book *The Three Robbers* to a class of five-year-olds. After reading the phrase 'searching for victims', I asked the children what 'victims' were. Only one child suggested that they were 'people that the robbers were looking for'. At the end of the story I asked the question again. Although the whole class had heard the explanation of victims, they had forgotten already. Even the original child who had understood from the context what victims were, no longer remembered when the support of the context was taken away. I do not advocate continually interrupting stories to explain meanings of words for, by and large, if the story is pitched right, the context will help children understand new words and, if the teacher feels that more explanation is necessary, she can expand the story gently to make things clearer. But asking such questions from time to time does a great deal to help the teacher's understanding of her children's learning and development.

A well-crafted tale

Well-written stories do not make linguistic concessions. They do not talk down to children. They succeed in putting over difficult language by subtly interweaving familiar and unfamiliar words and unnoticeably explaining things as they go along. A good example is the finely crafted children's story, *The Five Chinese Brothers,* by Claire Hutchet Bishop and Kurt Wiese. We are introduced to the Chinese brothers who have amazing attributes. One has 'an iron neck' – that's simple enough. Another 'could hold his breath indefinitely'. You may not be quite sure what 'indefinitely' means but it sounds impressive and the meaning becomes perfectly clear as the story develops. A phrase such as 'obey me promptly' might, on its own, stump a child in a reading test but in the text it is immediately followed by a clear explanation: 'When I make a sign for you to come back, you must come at once.' When the little boy in the story says not simply 'yes' but impatiently 'Yes Yes' you know that he has not taken in an 'imperative command'. Later on when the Chinese brother who 'could swallow the sea' is having trouble keeping it down, you may not know exactly what 'desperate gestures' are, but the pictures make it pretty clear how anxious he is to beckon the little boy back. The little boy is too preoccupied with the sea bed and its 'strange pebbles, extraordinary shells and fantastic algae'. It matters little that you do not know the meaning of every word, the poetic sense comes over. Even though the words and expressions may well be immediately forgotten following the reading or telling of such a story, they will be better recognized when next met. The sum of all the recollections of words and all the ways they can be put together will help the young reader make them part of his own language, to the point where he can use it as well as understand it, and even go on to understand and employ 'style'. I can think of no better way of language development than the unconscious absorption of well-written stories. Manufactured efforts at so-called 'language development' are far inferior because they are so artificial and self conscious and of course, are not at all concerned with style.

Psychological accuracy and an eye for detail

Story books help a child's language to grow. They can also provide general knowledge in an especially vivid way and put it in a human context. In this sense, a well-told tale is worth a thousand information books in being able to suggest what things are really like. This can be true, however improbable the story, when it is as carefully observed and truthful as, say, one of the 'Little Tim' stories by Edward Ardizzone. *Little Tim and the Brave Sea Captain* tells a most unlikely story of Tim going to sea as a stowaway and being rescued after a storm. But, within its daydream framework, the book is accurate in details about ships and the sea. Like all good children's stories it can be enjoyed by adults at another level. As a stowaway, Tim encounters a mixture of callousness and comradeship which one imagines is, or was, characteristic of the sea-going life.

In fact Tim is ruthlessly exploited as a skivvy and there is a convincing scene where he gets into his bunk too tired to take off his clothes. Before they are rescued, Tim and the Captain are resigned to the fact they are 'bound for Davy Jones's Locker and tears won't help us now'. Even though Tim is not quite sure where Davy Jones's locker is, his behaviour is a model of bravery. It is only much later, when he is kissed by ladies who give him chocolate and fruit, that Tim 'cannot help feeling a bit of a hero'. This psychological accuracy seems even more important for children to learn that the nicely salty language of 'stowing gear', 'working your passage', 'tidying the galley', 'lifeboats coming alongside' and so on.

Another nice touch is at the beginning of the story, where Tim astonishes his parents with his detailed observations of ships: 'a Cunarder', or a 'barquentine on the port bow'. When their interest is aroused children are capable of amassing facts with ease. Good stories prompt this fact-gathering and then help shape the facts into a coherent view of their 'whys and wherefores'. We neglect the imaginative use of language at our peril. George Orwell has shown in his famous novel *1984* how, when language is reduced, thought is reduced, and tyranny is exercized by means of 'Newspeak' which compresses all language into expressions of official approval or disapproval.

Moral lessons

Often teachers are frustrated when individual children want to ask a lot of questions and to get deeply into a story or a character, but the needs of the class as a whole must prevail. This is where parents have the great advantage which they should always seize, not simply in order to advance their children's factual learning: their moral education and knowledge of human nature is also improved. Since we reacted against the Victorians' blatant and unctuous moralizing at children, we have leaned over backwards to avoid drawing a moral from stories. Yet a lot of children's stories contain sound lessons about morals and behaviour which teachers and parents should not be afraid of applying.

The success of Dorothy Edward's *My Naughty Little*

Sister stories rests upon the young listener feeling deliciously superior to the unfailingly mischievous little sister who does all the things that they have precariously grown out of. 'My naughty little sister' walks into the water with her shoes and socks on, eats everyone else's sandwiches and spills lemonade at a picnic, refuses everything offered to her for breakfast, won't help a bit when she is being dressed, and 'you know what that means', and digs up the flower bed. In effect, these stories congratulate young children on their hard-won *savoir faire* and new ability to subdue over-excited, frightened and egotistical reactions. 'My naughty little sister's' most shocking crime is to bite Father Christmas's hand at a school party when she has been made to wait for her present. This is a truly horrifying incident for five-year-olds, who have only just mastered their own deep desire to bite people who annoy them.

There are straightforwardly moral tales which children enjoy and can profit from linguistically as well as morally. *Aesop's Fables* remain in a class of their own. Dr Seuss's parable of the Sneetches is a modern classic. The 'star belly sneetches' lord it over the 'plain belly sneetches,' until Sylvester McMonkey McBean, the 'fix it up chappie,' gets rich quick by alternately fixing and removing stars. The Sneetches learn an expensive lesson about the need to live together in spite of slight physical differences. In the same book is what I consider the best Seuss parable, a story of a hero haunted by a pair of pale green pants with nobody inside them, which helps any child to come to terms with his irrational fears.

> 'I do not fear those pants with nobody inside them'
> I said and said those words
> I said them but I lied them!

In the end, of course, the hero learns the green pants are

just as scared of him. The final confrontation creates an unforgettable image, 'those spooky empty pants and I were standing face to face'.

Fact and fantasy

The Schools Council study of children's reading noted that in all the books most popular with the young reader there was at least one character with whom he could be expected to associate himself emotionally. The authors went on to quote Sigmund Freud's description of the playing child and the poet both wishing to transpose the world 'according to an arrangement which is more to their liking', and further to quote the Bullock Report's advice that we should guide the young reader towards experience which enlarge his understanding of the range of human possibilities.

I feel educationists sometimes handle the question of emotional identification in too narrow and utilitarian a fashion. It has become the vogue to provide young children with heavy doses of social realism in their early reading, as if the up-to-date version of *Little Tim and the Brave Sea Captain* should be *Little Tim and the Friendly Supermarket Manager*. Children are equally at home with fact and fantasy as long as the story is good. Neither realism for its own sake nor adult whimsy unsupported by a well-crafted story have any appeal for children.

Children under six years of age make little distinction between fantasy and reality in stories. The world is a place where anything can happen, so they are unlikely to be surprised by any of the goings on in stories. Leila Berg's retelling of the folk tales *Rabbit and Elephant* is an excellent illustration of their open-mindedness. In this story Elephant goes off into the long grass in order to undo the sixteen buttons of his grey coat and reappear as a purple striped monster that will frighten Rabbit. Very young children are not in the least surprised that an elephant's grey coat is an outer garment. But most of them do not even recognize the purple striped monster as the elephant without his grey skin. After the age of six, children become more concerned with the likelihood and probability of things. Is it true? Could it really happen? They may react scathingly to a far-fetched story. Once they come to understand the story-telling conventions, children take each story on its merits, and learn to apply them in stories they write themselves.

10 Immigrant Children

Racial and cultural identity

Immigrant children present a special teaching problem where reading and writing are concerned. Although complex, it is by no means insoluble, providing it is carefully analyzed and well meaning but superficial solutions are avoided. In the first instance we have to use the phrase 'immigrant children' to describe children of quite varying circumstances, many of whom may not be immigrants at all but born in this country, some of them to parents who themselves were born here. Nevertheless, most of the parents are of overseas origin who have retained their racial and cultural identity.

The main groups are West Indians, Asians from the Indian sub-continent, and Cypriots. There are some minorities of Chinese, Asians from Africa, and Africans themselves. For economic and social reasons, the majority of immigrants tend to collect together in poor areas of inner cities and towns, and, for a mixture of geographical and social reasons, their children tend to congregate within the same schools in these areas. Racial prejudice has nothing directly to do with the way immigrant children fare in learning to read, but culture, language, economics, social environment, and living conditions all affect reading and writing, usually for the worse. Surveys have shown that immigrant children do generally less well in school than the indigenous population.

Things will get better

The Bullock Report, while mentioning the lack of sustained research into the comparative performance of children of minority groups in school in Britain, summarizes the disturbing results of surveys carried out in London and Birmingham. For example, in the Inner London Education area (which in 1972 had nearly a quarter of all the immigrant children in school in England and Wales), twenty-nine per cent of immigrant children were poor readers compared with fifteen per cent of non-immigrants. However, for reasons which I will explain, such figures have to be approached with great care. On the one hand, things are changing and teachers are learning from their experience, on the other hand there are important differences between the various minority groups which are obscured by averages. I do not think I am falsely optimistic in saying things will get better as the often painfully acquired experience of teachers of immigrant children born in this country increases.

Teachers have had to feel their way in devising new philosophies for dealing with immigrant children and coping with the difficulties created at every turn by cultural and language differences. It has been an ill wind that has blown good by the growth of 'ghetto schools' in which teachers could get used to large groups of immigrant children, whether of a single minority or as a mixture. I have noticed that in schools with only a handful of immigrant children, teachers have adapted much more slowly.

Drawbacks of language

Real as some of the technical difficulties are, it must not be overlooked that the very tests which show poorer performance by immigrants are insidiously loaded against them. Children who may be reasonably fluent in English may attach different meanings, or no meaning at all, to 'common' English words and expressions. I was reminded that language can never be taken for granted with children of other cultures when I read a class of seven-year-olds, of mixed races, the story of *Jemima Puddleduck*. The stupid duck invited to a dinner party by the fox is unperturbed by his request for her to bring along 'some sage for the stuf...' he starts to say. The joke was completely lost on the children, who had never had sage and onion stuffing – not even from a packet. In discussion they were free with suggestions as to how best to cook a fowl in pilaff, curry, stew, etc.

The teacher of immigrant children, therefore, cannot take very much as 'read'. The first and most obvious thing she cannot assume is a child's ability to speak English. Asian and Cypriot children may arrive speaking no English at all. As quite often the parents are also without English, the problem starts with enrolment. I have known Asian tots bravely turn up on their own hoping to join the school but unable to communicate until an interpreter is found. More often they come with a slightly older sister, brother or friend. And yet the difficulties are not so acute with an absolute beginner in the early years of primary school. If a non-English-speaking child learns to read and write soon after starting school, along with everyone else, he will be slow but will eventually catch up. If he has the innate ability he will overtake his classmates. The worries arise with older, non-English-speaking children who cannot take part in a normal curriculum until they have fully learned to read and write.

The most proficient teachers of English

It would seem logical and indeed humane to put such children in a special class on their own. In fact, this would be the worst thing that could happen to them. The next worst thing would be for them to find themselves in a rigidly formal class where the main activity was written exercises. In both instances they would be cut off from their most proficient teachers of English, the other children. In an informal classroom, free to talk and move about and make things together, they quickly learn to speak our language and understand its conventions. Even children who do not speak English at home will, with the right stimulus of creative activities, toys and friends, be able to learn English in about a year.

Nonetheless, coping with two languages and the slowing down of learning of English at weekends and in the holidays, make for a considerable handicap which teachers and administrators must allow for. They should remember that the bilingual child is fortunate. Slower performance in written English and reading tests must be balanced against his wider achievement in learning two languages.

The intolerable distress that some non-English-speaking children show on starting school may persuade a teacher that they need special and separate teaching. Concern at their being pitch-forked from one culture into another may make a teacher feel that they should have specially tailored materials. This would be misguided. The answer to both problems is a normal curriculum at a slower pace, plus a more emphatic style of teaching. Teachers with non-English-speaking children in the class need to employ more dramatic gestures and facial expressions until they are sure of being understood. At first it might seem inappropriate to include non-English-speaking children in the audience for story-telling, but what more valuable way is there of helping them learn English? The trick is to use a heightened style, to have accompanying pictures, to act out and mime parts of the story, and to go for stories with repetitive language and plot. With such techniques the non-English-speaking child is no worse off in story-telling than you or I at the opera.

Stored knowledge

Other useful methods for non-English-speaking children are rhymes and fingerplays, and materials such as the pre-reader or caption books described earlier, with the same basic sentence repeated on every page. Although the prime purpose in using caption books at this stage is to familiarize children with the English language by focusing on simple statements, many non-English-speaking children do begin reading in this way.

What it all comes down to is that you cannot learn a language in a vacuum, but neither can you learn it in an artificially programmed way. I have noticed that in schools where special English language classes were oversub-scribed, the non-English-speaking children who had to stay in normal classes on that account, actually learned English much more quickly. Their first spoken words may not have been in the most elegant phrasing – more likely remarks such as 'I'll bash you up' or 'Miss, Jason's hitting me,' statements borne of necessity and learned from other children, not from the teacher. I once taught a little Turkish boy who had not spoken any English. One day in assembly a little girl piped up with a request for a Christmas carol. I explained that as it was April it was not really the proper time to sing a song about Christmas. 'It no Christmas', shouted Salim, and fell about with laughter. He had carefully listened and stored all his knowledge about Christmas and carols and then, after months of apparent unconcern, he suddenly showed his awareness.

A silent frozen classroom, still found in some formal schools, is an unhelpful place for children with limited English. They will get along better in the more responsive atmosphere of an informal classroom, but there is no getting away from the arithmetic that allows only a few minutes of the teacher's time on average for each individual child per day. So, if it is at all possible, ancillary helpers and parents should be brought in to chat to, and listen sympathetically to, non-English-speaking children.

Children entering school in an older age group will definitely need short periods of intensive help with spoken English as well as remedial work to help them catch up with their classmates. While there are a number of special materials and programmes available for the teaching of English as a second language, it does not greatly matter what the teacher uses as long as she involves the children in interesting activities and encourages them to talk. I have found the experiments in primary science (for example 'Nuffield Science Five to Thirteen'), one of the best ways of teaching English.

There is no basis for anxiety about teaching children to read and write at the same time as teaching them spoken language. In my observation, understanding English precedes the ability to speak it. Quite often children who are shy of speaking English, probably through fear of making a mistake and being laughed at, develop confidence in reading aloud other people's prose. It can be objected that children who can read but remain inarticulate do not understand what they are reading. Even if this is true, I feel that they are learning something of the mechanics of reading, and usually they understand far more than they show. If you question any child on what he has read, he may not be able to recall or explain what it is about, but this does not mean he has not understood. Being able to answer questions and give a resumé of what has been read, are quite advanced skills which are independent of reading itself. With this in mind, I believe it is worthwhile digressing to a certain extent in order to discuss what has become known as 'language development'.

Self-consciousness about language

The supporters of this notion advocate a highly planned

approach to language learning. They are really the succes-
sors of the old-fashioned grammarians, convinced that
language is a complex mechanism which cannot be operated by the unwary. Once you might have been stopped in
your tracks by the knowledge that you were speaking prose
and had better learn to parse it. Nowadays, it seems, you
cannot get by without 'vocabulary building', 'sentence
patterns', 'problem solving' and 'concept formation'–
such being the ingredients of the Peabody Language
Development Kit. Another language development programme deals in the 'giving and repeating of instructions',
and 'use of comparisons and choices', and 'relational
words'. Yet another programme sets out to improve speech
in respect of 'extended narrative', 'explanation', 'detailed
description', 'expression of uncertainty' and the 'hypo-
thetical description of feeling and relationships'. This self-
consciously portentous approach to language has had
several interesting but unprofitable consequences. One of
them has been the proliferation of commercial 'language
laboratories' and other associated language developments,
resting upon the discovery that teachers were hardly more
award than their charges of the cogs and ratchets whirring
away within the mechanism of language. Teachers have
been urged to become more analytically conscious of
language procedures. For example, recording conversa-
tions with children in order to appraise their use of
language. From there it is a short step to a linguistic regime
in which 'skills' count for more than ability and the means
have submerged the ends. In my opinion, these ideas
should never have left the laboratory.

What I have against them, apart from the jargon, is that
they get in the way of direct teaching of language. They
encourage the belief that 'language' is a subject in its own
right. They deny the appreciation of language as something organic, personal and highly versatile that is part of
our whole existence. They make ordinary teachers too self-

conscious in speaking about language. I have before me the policy document of a primary school which includes a chart of the 'language environment', with arrows pointing to such things as 'peer group interaction', 'parent teacher dialogue', 'interaction in viability of material and awareness', 'intrinsically motivating' and 'home community school'. It would be impossible to make up any of this, or concoct such phrases as the 'ability to cooperate in meaningful interaction', 'projecting teacher child relationships' and 'the opportunity to extend and express situations'. I lay the blame for such rubbish at the door of the self-proclaimed experts who clutter the educational world. I shudder to think that such phrases might have been taken from the notes of an education lecture.

A closer look at the survey results

My comments on the difficulties caused by lack of English, and the poor reading performance figure quoted earlier for minority groups, could easily give the impression that language – linguistic difference – was the heart of the problem. A closer look at the survey results produces an opposite conclusion. Bullock quotes an unpublished analysis of all Inner London Education Authority pupils transferring to secondary schools. It showed that among the immigrant children who were fully educated in this country, those of Asian origin did as well as indigenous children. However, children of West Indian origin performed well below average. Similar disturbing findings come from other surveys mentioned. Because such findings bear so harshly upon one particular group they tend to get obscured by generalizations about the language difficulties of immigrant children who are 'multiply disadvantaged'. But lack of English is a minor factor in the poorer

performance of West Indian children. Nowadays few of
them enter British schools directly from the West Indies.
Most of them were born here, often as second generation
native. Most of the ones I have come across speak English
with a local accent. The difficulties created for those
children who do speak a West Indian dialect, or use
idiosyncratic words and expressions kept alive among
West Indians in this country, should not be overlooked. Yet
all children are accustomed to coping with the contrast
between a private language formed by local speech patterns, and the received speech and written language the
school uses. Schools in the West Indies do not use a *patois*
for reading and writing texts. So it is a little surprising that
the Schools Council project found that dialect problems
impeded children's learning of English in respect of 'oral
comprehension', 'spoken intelligibility', reading, writing
and spelling (*Teaching English to West Indian Children*).

Whatever might have been the problem in the early days
of West Indian immigration, it seems clear to me that now
a West Indian child is no more at a disadvantage with his
intonation than a child from Yorkshire or Scotland in a
Cockney classroom.

I acknowledge that cultural differences can impede
learning to read and write, just as certain attitudes to dress
affect physical education, and attitudes to gender restrict
female advancement. I have already pointed out that
ignorance of vocabulary and concepts can cause immigrant
children to perform less well than they ought in reading
tests (although this is equally true for indigenous children
of limited culture and experience). Nonetheless, the evidence exists that Asians, whose culture is most widely
removed from our own, are perfectly competent at learning to read and write in the primary school. We know that
West Indian culture is closer to our own. If language and
cultural background are not critical factors, where should
we look for the answer?

A possible failure of identification

People have criticized the books used for teaching reading in our schools, for not portraying coloured children or reflecting the immigrants' way of life. Do West Indian children in particular fail to identify with the characters they are reading about? Even if this lack of balance could be corrected overnight, I doubt it would make much difference. The quality of a book is far more important than the inclusion of coloured people in the text and illustrations. Immigrant children are as critical of poor literature as any other children. Most of the books specially produced for so-called multiracial education are self-conscious and worthily superficial. If children were less trusting, they would feel insultingly patronized. One answer to the problem of reading books appearing too parochial these days is to cast the net more widely in the choice of genuinely 'universal' literature. This search sends us happily back to the many traditional tales that call up no national or racial references. (Although there is an unfortunate tendency in some tales from Northern Europe to cast heroines as white-skinned, golden-haired and beautiful, while black is frequently associated with evil.)

The National Book League has produced helpful lists of books which portray immigrant children, and the School Libraries Association has put out a similar list of children's books showing the background of India, Pakistan and the West Indies (addresses at the back of the book). As the world shrinks while becoming no better behaved, such books ought to be of interest to all teachers and parents. But the choice of a moral message should never be put ahead of a 'good read'.

Family influences

Most teachers who deal with immigrant children are aware

that ethnic factors strongly influence a child's sense of
security. Asian and Cypriot families are usually tightly
knit. They are eager to maintain their cultural identity and
set great store by family life. Although linguistically this
would appear a handicap, family pride acts as a positive
influence on the child's academic achievement, including
facility with English – the classic key to success of the
immigrant. West Indian families, who appear to start with
all the advantages of a broadly British culture (and fluency
in an unusual but perfectly valid English dialect) in general
give less encouragement to reading and writing. There is
less marital stability, which is often attributed to a social
pattern laid down during the period of slavery. Against a
looser family background, West Indian children's achievement is determined by their position on the bottom rung of
the socio-economic ladder. Their parents are forced into
the lowest paid jobs and the most rudimentary living
accommodation. The combination of parents working long
hours and the poor domestic and social environment
frequently produces an educational handicap. The worst
aspect of this is the way in which West Indian children are
often left with unregistered childminders. Just when
children should be benefiting from gentle affection and the
beginnings of social and academic education, they may be
forced to spend long barren hours without attention or
distraction. Even when children are attending school, they
may have to look after themselves in the morning without
any parental help in dressing and making breakfast; and
after school return home to an empty dwelling for several
hours before their parents come home from work.

West Indian children are well-cared for physically; they
are well-fed and well-dressed, but their parents have to
work long hours to maintain those standards. When the
parents come home in the evening they face the household
chores and probably feel too tired or lack the time to read to
their children, to tell them stories and rhymes, to take an

interest in their school work and help them with it, and to talk to them. I have come reluctantly to the conclusion that one of the main reasons for West Indian children's poorer performance in school is the lack of personal attention from too busy parents. This may be the explanation for the lack of fluency in language and the characteristic attention-seeking behaviour, such as temper tantrums.

My analysis may be unfair to West Indian parents, but at least it is more encouraging than the vaguely racist implication of the statistics, that West Indian children are inherently inferior. For the positive lesson is that children who are emotionally and intellectually neglected, as well as those who lack linguistic stimulation, would benefit from nursery education and pre-school playgroups. It seems to me that immigrant children must be given absolute priority in providing such resources and in overcoming a simple barrier. Too often part-time, pre-school places are made available without any regard for the fact that the children who might benefit are locked into childminding arrangements. The minders cannot afford to take children to and from school twice a day for half their usual fee. The parents hesitate to pay the minder for the time the children are at nursery school. I notice that, wherever there are part-time nurseries, they are under-used. Yet there is a constant demand for full-time nursery places.

The benefits of a good start

Inner city teachers who are most aware of the problems of immigrant children bless the advantages conferred on a child by a nursery school or playgroup preparation. They do not do this for reasons of selfish convenience. Primary teachers are aware that their pupils have their entire careers before them and will develop at different rates. Nonetheless a good start benefits every child and when basic social and linguistic skills have been encouraged by the parents or by pre-school teachers, the three R's will be learned more smoothly, creative work will come more easily, and playing and working together as a class will happen as a matter of course.

West Indian children are also at risk educationally from their more boisterous personalities. They seem less able to concentrate on quiet work. They need to move about more, to play more and generally to let off steam. Lest I be misunderstood, I should say that I find these qualities attractive and stimulating, for I am an advocate of informal, lively classrooms. It just so happens that the traditional classroom, silent, and without surprise or stimulus, is anathema to most West Indian children. Likewise a noisy, uncontrolled, undisciplined classroom spells educational disaster for them. Both sets of circumstances lead to problems of discipline. The time spent in sorting out behavioural difficulties is teaching time wasted and so adds to deprivation. Gradually, however, the seemingly insoluble problems of discipline have been solved by teachers coming to terms with racial characteristics and environmental effects. People do not dwell on the fact that life is more difficult for teachers in schools with a large immigrant population. As such schools tend to be in the poorer parts of large cities they are less attractive to staff. By and large the teachers who have been willing to join such schools have been dedicated enough but inexperienced and transitory. I am sure the high teacher turnover in recent years has penalized immigrant children, especially West Indians. There has been an unfortunate clash of young teachers, making their characteristic beginners' mistakes, and immigrant children, making their characteristic mistakes. The result; a general lack of reassurance and understanding. Many of the teachers concerned very quickly found their feet, but just as they were beginning to cope with the problems of the muti-racial classroom and even opening their staider colleagues' eyes to some of the possibilities, they would move on to the greener suburbs. For the past few years teacher turnover has dropped, and young teachers seem more willing to put in a longer stint. Immigrant children are bound to benefit from the greater stability and know-how that multi-racial schools have acquired. Gradually, immigrant children are becoming more self-assured. Faced with today's lurid stories of racial conflict I am consoled that in the primary school classroom it is much diminished. I should be upset if an educational backlash produced rigidly formal classrooms in which for the reasons I have described, immigrant children were left floundering and resentful.

11 Remedial Reading

Late starting is not a problem

Reading has its quick and its slow learners, as with any subject. But reading is not simply a body of knowledge to be worked steadily through. For the quicker the grasp of reading, the faster the acceleration of learning to read; thus the more widespread the benefit in other kinds of instruction. The slower the grasp of reading, the quicker the rate at which difficulties and discouragements spring up. The distance that opens up between the front runners and the stragglers can become quite remarkable. Add to this arithmetic of learning the entirely natural way in which children achieve the knack of reading at different ages and stages of maturity and you can see that in the most 'normal' classroom there will be a very wide range of reading ability. It will be a teaching challenge but ought not to lead to worries about the children who are at the back of the field. There always seems to be plenty of time for catching up. Until children are about seven, there is no need for the slightest anxiety about inability to read. Parents of young children must show patience and never betray anxiety if their offspring seem not to take to reading at first. Parents who worry at all about the academic performance of their young children at school would do well to remember that in some countries their children would still be too young for school. In Norway, for example, children do not start school until the age of six.

This late start does not prevent them from learning to read, often in English as well as their native language.

Inability to read and slowness of learning are not necessarily signs of low intelligence. Some bright children have great difficulty with reading, to the point where pathological causes are suspected. Perhaps because of this, remedial reading has taken on a somewhat clinical image. While I am in favour of using any method to free children who have got stuck in their reading, I do not believe there is a qualitative difference between normal teaching of reading and remedial teaching. In the great majority of cases the remedy for poor reading is not a specific medicine but a more nourishing diet. In practice this means more books, more teachers, and more time spent.

The need for co-operation between infants and juniors

Because slow reading only becomes a serious problem after the age of eight, remedial teaching is mostly associated with junior classes. Unfortunately this may mean that the problem is tackled with less suitable material and fewer teachers experienced in beginning reading. Junior teachers may show impatience and resentment at the intrusion of remedial reading into the normal timetable.

It follows that remedial reading is an area where there should be full co-operation between an infant and a junior school. Yet a study by Joyce Morris showed the disturbing facts that seventy-six per cent of junior school teachers in a survey sample had received no training in infant methods and eighteen per cent had no knowledge of how to teach children to read (Joyce Morris, *Reading in the Primary School*). Similarly, an Inner London Education Authority survey showed that two-thirds of junior schools had no teacher who 'had received specific detailed training...to teach reading at training college or specialist course' (*Literacy Survey*, I.L.E.A.). Although these surveys were carried out a few years ago, there are no signs that things have improved. There is still a tendency for junior schools to expect reading to have been taken care of by the infant school. Once more the fault lies in a simplistic belief that reading is a once and for all achievement of the skill of 'decoding'. There is also little appreciation that a statistically average reading age of seven is no great shakes. It includes a perfectly normal band of children whose reading age is well below seven. Even if we were to fulfil the dreams of the politicians who look forward to the day when every child's reading age is above average, a top infant's reading ability is simply not good enough to cope. Therefore there is a double danger if junior school teachers are insufficiently thoughtful and informed in their attitude to reading. First, they will see their task as mainly remedial, perhaps leading them to a preoccupation with pathology. Secondly, they will fail to develop and polish the rudimentary reading skills acquired in the infant school.

Preventive measures in the infant school

Having called for a greater awareness by junior schools of their responsibility for keeping up the teaching of reading, I must emphasize the infants schools' responsibility for preventive measures. I know from experience that where there are extra reading teachers without class responsibilities, nearly every child will have made a good start in reading by the age of seven. After the beginning stage a child's reading performance will be directly proportional to the time spent reading. The motivation that comes from a successful beginning will have to be supplemented by a good choice of reading matter that a child can enjoy on his own.

In my observation, personality has a good deal more to do with ability to read than intelligence. Perseverance, patience, concentration and determination all help children of quite modest ability to become good readers. The plodding tortoise can sometimes pass the temperamental hare who cannot face even the possibility of failure. However, powers of concentration are limited in small children: some cannot even sit still long enough to concentrate on a patient activity such as reading. The skill of the teacher lies in planning the class timetable so as to give the fidgets frequent and short bursts of reading tuition. But the best form of learning to read demands fairly lengthy sessions, and it is a sad fact that children who cannot cope with these will tend to fall behind their fellows. On this account it is not surprising that boys find learning to read more difficult than do girls.

The view from the playground

This difference between boys and girls is the most important clue we have to reading failure. Whenever academic attainment is measured, males always seem to occupy a wide range of ability from the very poor to the very good, while females tend to cluster more into a middle band of ability. This may rest on sexual differences of behaviour and attitude, whether inherited or conditioned. Boys are more physically active, keener on what child psychologists call 'large muscle' activities and more easily distracted by their playmates. At the infant level this difference is extremely marked and perhaps accounts for the fact that girls are academically superior to boys in their early school years. Every day in the infant playground you will see boys rushing, pushing, fighting and playing in gangs, while girls are more likely to be seen round the edges, playing quieter and sometimes more solitary games. It is significant that girls are more interested in personal skills such as skipping (which surely is in no way sexual but does not seem to appeal to boys) and intricate handball games which are again of little concern to boys, who prefer to kick a big football round. Arguments are irrelevant here: even if sex role stereotyping could be abolished overnight, the same playground pattern would be repeated, based on personality types. (I believe myself that it comes down to physiology and musculature). The technical problem remains of teaching reading to children who are not inclined to mental activity and 'close up' skills.

Does dyslexia exist?

When children's reading difficulties seem to defy 'normal' explanations the word 'dyslexia' is often brought in. This term appears constantly in press articles about reading failure and has aroused a lot of controversy. I find dyslexia a question-begging word (its literal meaning, from the Greek, is 'poor reading'). The 'normal' explanations of reading failure include 'low intelligence', a home background of physical and mental poverty, physiological problems such as deafness and poor eyesight, and ill health in general. In some ways, dyslexia is a reflection of the distress felt by middle-class parents when their otherwise healthy and intelligent child demonstrates a chronic inability to read and write. At the same time, it is reassuring to such people that their problem is recognized and the unnecessary social stigma attached to illiteracy is removed. However, sticking a 'scientific' label on a problem does not go very far towards explaining its cause.

It may yet turn out that dyslexia is the result of a 'delayed maturation of the co-ordinating processes of the nervous system', as has been suggested, but I deplore the thought of teachers sitting back feeling that nothing can be done, especially when the term is used loosely of any unexpectedly retarded reader. I prefer to act on the assumption that no child is beyond help; I am heartened by the fact, mentioned earlier, that among dyslexics boys outnumber girls by five to one, which seems to bring us back to personality differences. If I am right, then positive practical help is possible in most cases.

The need for a reading model

The question is perhaps not posed often enough as to why a very young child should want to learn to read. A child needs to learn a spoken language in order to communicate. He sees that he can get along very nicely without the written language. The real benefits of reading and writing are in the future. The tedium and the effort of learning to read and write compete with many more exciting things. Teachers and parents must supply the competing motivation. But it is no use pointing to future advantages; small children live purely for the present. Yet where they do unconsciously prepare themselves for the future is in their desire to imitate adults. They want to do grown-up things. What teachers and parents must do, therefore, is to let children see them reading and writing; share these activities with their children and demonstrate that reading and writing are enjoyable and purposeful.

In those areas where most children come from bookless homes in which reading and writing have little 'perceived value', teachers must redouble their efforts to make reading appear enjoyable and purposeful. This point is underlined by recent statistics from studies by local education authorities in the North-west. In certain schools, serving the cultural deserts we call 'rehousing areas', twenty per cent of children were non-readers at the age of eight and another forty per cent were of very limited reading ability.

The need for constant encouragement

As well as wanting to imitate adults, young children want

to please them. Children in the beginning stages of reading may well read just to please the teacher and to show off newly acquired skills. For that reason it is vital that teachers and parents respond with unqualified delight. A child who sees no particular point in reading, except as an adult game and to please grown-ups, will soon be put off by harsh criticism. Corrections should always be made gently and incidentally, and there should be little or no criticism. A child's parents and their friends respond with boundless joy when a child starts to walk and talk. Quite rightly. Would they dream of chastising an infant for not being able to talk properly at first? Parents always encourage their child by showing pleasure, showering praise, and joining in the game. Why then should we even contemplate changing the rules for the beginning reader? I would not deny that showing unalloyed pleasure upon every reading occasion can be wearisome for a teacher with a class of thirty or more. The toothpaste smile starts to slip a little. Teachers may sometimes be too distracted to confer the expected praise. Here is where parents can be most helpful, by providing the motivation that comes from their delight in the child's present achievements. Unfortunately parents' reaction is too often an impatient anxiety, a feeling of 'about time too' and an over-readiness to criticize. Even implied criticism of the school is taken personally by the child. This may be why some class teachers act defensively about reading, and discourage parents from helping, for fear their attitudes may do more harm than good.

Once more, the best way is to put parents as much as possible in the picture. The same advice applies to later stages of reading, when performance will be proportional to time spent. There are no laurels to rest on in reading: motivation has to be kept up with a supply of good books introduced to the child. We tend to underestimate the know-how it takes to choose books and to get the best out of them. Parents' help is invaluable here as well.

'We feel ashamed'

It will have become plain that I see reading failure as chiefly an absence of some or all of the conditions for success. An ounce of prevention is worth a ton of cure. I see a lot of remedial programmes as extra ambulances at the bottom of the cliff – I should like to see more fences at the top, more efforts made to capture the attention and interests of slow readers. As we know, many of them are highly active boys, and their difficulties must be anticipated by devoting more time to them in the early stages, and having suitable material ready to prevent their interest flagging. An act of faith is needed. I am sure that if local authorities provided extra staff to hear children read without distraction outside the classroom, we would not have so many reading failures at later stages. For failure breeds failure. Once a child feels he has fallen behind, he will try to avoid anything that reminds him of his failure. Children may feel branded by being selected for remedial help. This was brought home to me forcibly when a local nine-year-old came to my house and asked me to teach him to read. I inquired if he did not have a special teacher at his school who helped those children who couldn't read yet. 'Yes but we play her up.' 'Why do you do that if you want to learn to read?' 'I expect it's because we feel ashamed.'

The value of a home with books in it

Perhaps in the end one of the simplest reasons for reading failure is sheer lack of time devoted to teaching reading. I suggested earlier that parents could help by allowing ten minutes or so a day for helping their children with reading, a lot more than a teacher can allow on average. Of course, the parents who cannot be bothered to do this are also likely to be those who are not interested in books or even in education. However, parents who do want to help with reading will be heartened by the findings of Professor Stephen Wiseman (Plowden Report, Volume 2, Appendix 9) in a study of Manchester ten-year-olds. He carried out a statistical analysis of all the environmental factors that influence 'educational progress and attainment of primary school children'. He concluded that 'factors in the home are overwhelmingly more powerful than those of the neighbourhood and the school – and of these, factors of parental attitude to education, to the school and to books are of far greater significance than social class and occupational level.' If Professor Wiseman is right in his conclusion, a home with books in it is the surest guarantee of educational success – but this makes all the more poignant the cases of dyslexia. In such homes, where there are plenty of books, there are no magic formulae for guaranteed success. Nor is there any magic about remedial reading: it is based on 'more of the same'. There is no special technique that can be brought into play on behalf of the children who have seemed impervious to ordinary methods. The same ordinary methods have to be used on extra occasions with smaller groups of children working at a slower rate. A great deal depends then on the skill of the remedial teacher who must ring the changes on familiar themes. Remedial teaching demands a rather rare combination of patience, imagination and enthusiasm.

By and large the children who come to remedial classes will have been defeated by repetitive exercises and drills. They will respond better to jollier approaches, especially reading games which restore some fun to a seemingly difficult task.

The need for extra help

There is no set way in which schools deploy their remedial reading resources. A remedial teacher may have her own class or may withdraw groups of children from a normal class for short periods. The latter seems to be a better way, as it helps to stop children being permanently labelled as 'a backward stream'. Unfortunately some schools have neither the extra teacher nor a separate room for remedial reading classes. Since reading ability has such a strong bearing on nearly every other subject, it would seem a priority for every school to get a remedial teacher and classroom. Once such teachers were able to catch poor readers before they became hopeless cases, I am convinced reading backwardness would all but disappear from primary schools. My proposal may seem idealistic, but once the problem spills over into secondary school it becomes exacerbated, and more massive resources are needed to tackle it. By secondary school age children have become acutely aware of their failure and have already taken up defensive attitudes to compensate. Their ability to learn any language, which a child of six does unselfconsciously in a few months, has grown stiff.

It would be in everyone's interest if children could be screened so as to pick out those children in need of extra help. Although I advocate prevention rather than cure, I have to admit that there is no simple test to ensure that we can detect potential failures. (When the Bullock Committee invited 145 local authorities in England to tell them 'how they identified their children likely to experience reading and language difficulties', they discovered that pupils were tested at nine different ages between seven and fifteen, using twenty different tests and twenty-four different criteria of reading disability.) The only reliable way is for the teacher to decide which children are falling behind at any particular time, and shepherd them along. Teachers must use their judgement in this matter and not be seduced by psychological tests which purport to measure reading readiness and potential. It will be clear by now what my attitude is towards such concepts as 'visual acuity' and 'auditory discrimination' as predictors of reading ability. As Frank Smith puts it, any child who can see well enough to spear a pea with a fork can see well enough to read. Time spent on elaborate tests of reading skills would be better devoted to teaching.

12 Adult Illiterates

Outright failures

It is a matter of shame that after twelve years in our education system normal people can emerge unable to read and write well enough to take a full part in society. At a more pragmatic level, any philosophy of education is utterly vulnerable if it can have its failures flung in its face. There is no use our being simply compassionate and enthusiastic on behalf of adult illiterates. We must try and learn from their plight.

Illiterates are cut off from most jobs and from promotion in the jobs they do get. They are increasingly at a disadvantage in our bureaucratic society. Would that someone could put an end to all the forms for income tax, VAT, social security, electoral registers, planning permission, rent rebates, free school dinners, farming subsidies, driving licences, job applications and so on, that even highly literate people have difficulty with! In the meantime illiterate people have to rely on others to cope with official forms and, if they run a business, with all the bookkeeping as well. This may lead to feelings of anxiety. For many illiterates their inability is a guilty secret that they will go to any lengths to dissemble. When I recently had the opportunity of teaching adult illiterates, I felt I should test my own hypothesis about why children fail in reading and writing, and see exactly what had become of these failures by the time they were adults.

It seemed to me that the chief reason for failure among

adult illiterates was failure itself. Just as a child who has decided reading success is beyond him will avoid situations carrying the slightest risk of failure, so these adults have long been on a slippery slope that has carried them away from any possibility of achievement. They cannot be euphemistically labelled as 'slow learners'. They are outright failures and carry a social stigma resulting from the high value society has put on reading and writing. While anyone can proudly boast that he hasn't a clue with figures, or has no ear for music, or can't read a chemical equation, or hates sport, or can't make head nor tail of modern art, you'll never hear anyone saying he can't read a word, or do you mind if he signs with an 'X'. In the circumstances it is brave of any illiterate to try again.

The status of education and literacy

However, it also seemed to me that the social value of literacy was waning. It has become a lot easier to be indifferent to reading and writing ability. This attitude reflects the declining status of teachers and of education itself: the economic motivation for a good education can hardly stand up to the lessening of wage differentials. The part once played by sustained reading of books has been taken over for many people by T.V., and it is hard to see how affection for the printed word could be nourished again in such households. The audio-visual media are always ready to proclaim that books and newspapers are dying. The third force weakening the status of education and literacy is the social change that has broken up communities and fragmented families. A typical outcome of lonely, high-rise living and one-parent families is the mother who keeps the school age child at home, setting a greater value on his company and usefulness in running errands than on schooling.

Perhaps the keenest impression that comes from dealing

with adult illiterates is that they wasted their best learning time, those key years in early childhood when a child can learn a language, or a manual skill such as writing, within a year or two. This is partly to do with a receptive brain but is also a matter of attitude – the small child's unconscious assumption that anything is possible. Once self-consciousness intrudes, learning can become painful, as many adults who have tried to learn a foreign language will confirm.

What happens when the novelty wears off

Illiterates face a forbidding task. I am glad they now benefit from government funds, encouragement from brilliant B.B.C teaching material, and the enthusiasm of the press, education authorities, teachers and volunteer helpers. Yet I feel we are in danger of underestimating just what uphill work it is. We marvel at a small child's capacity to learn to read and write in just a few years, but we expect to train grown-ups for a few hours a week, sustain them when the novelty wears off, track them down when they give up, and provide them with a powerful personal motivation for teaching themselves at home. We have to play down the fact that a lot of the material is babyish; that a primary school classroom is not the most inspiring location (in that they are being re-taught at the scene of their previous failure); and that certain of the volunteer helpers may be more of a hindrance than a help. The heart of the matter is that teacher and taught in literacy classes often labour under the belief that there is a simple key that will unlock the reading problem in a very short time. This belief is often associated with the mastery of phonics. It is indeed an attractive notion that all you need do is provide the student with a number of phonic rules which enable him to work out for himself how to read and write. In practice, the reader who has failed before is least likely to have the mental capacity for analysis and synthesis which allows brighter children to make faster progress with the aid of phonics. I have reluctantly come to the conclusion that you cannot teach people to read with only brief periods of teaching a week. If a person has failed to learn the basis of education after twenty-five hours per week in the classroom (amounting to ten or eleven thousand hours in a school career), it is asking a lot to remedy matters in an hour or two a week. I should dearly like my pessimism to be refuted by figures demonstrating the widespread success of the current literacy programme. I have yet to come across such evidence.

My pessimism about adult illiterates may appear at odds with my optimistic claims that nearly every child is capable of learning to read. However, since I believe that anyone's proficiency in reading and writing will depend on the time he spends on it and the amount of effort put into independent practice, it appears more logical. If an adult illiterate accepts this, and is not discouraged by the need to go back almost to the beginning and to put in far more than two hours a week, keeping it up for years if necessary, I shall be optimistic about his chances.

Parallels with children learning to read

Among the adult illiterates I came across there were types who corresponded to slow learners among children. There were the ones who would be successful in the end because they were highly motivated and determined. But the majority were erratic attenders, corresponding to poor attenders (in both sense of the word) in the school classroom. A proportion never returned after the holidays. Others were assiduous but, perhaps through some fault of personality or intellect, were trapped in their own faulty learning tactics. For example, one student could never get away from his ingrained habit of laboriously sounding out each word letter by letter, and so failed to pick up any thread of meaning whatsoever. There was another who was fluent with a handful of words which he resolutely refused to depart from. In a way they parodied the more unimaginative aspects of early reading drill. I need not paint too gloomy a picture as there were many successes in our classes, but I have to admit that these were mainly immigrants who were not, strictly speaking, adult illiterates, and who had mastered their own language well enough. They seemed to enjoy learning to read and write in English. The lessons I brought away from this experience reinforced my belief in the importance of material, motivation and continuity.

Often people are poor readers not because they find learning too hard, but because they find forgetting too easy. Illiterates and semi-literates avoid contact with print, so forgetting the little they have learned. Teachers are familar with the dramatic forgetting that can occur in the school holidays. When the relapse becomes permanent the deterioration of poor readers is as bad as most of us might experience in, for example, looking at a passage of Latin which we might have understood with ease at the age of fifteen. I feel the remedy for adult illiterates and all poor readers must lie in daily practice. I would urge such people to buy a newspaper every day, even if they read only a small part. If schools could advise the less able school leavers to do that, they might not slip back so far as to damage their job prospects and social dealings.

A learning plateau

Those of us who compared notes about teaching adult illiterates were strongly aware of a 'plateau' in their learning. Their rate of learning rose steeply at first, then flattened out until it seemed from week to week that they were making no progress. The possible reason for this, some tutors thought, was that we had spent the time bringing these students up to the standard of their highest achievement at school. Alternative hypotheses were that the student had reached his own intellectual limitations or had reached the barrier represented by the vocabulary demands of any text beyond the 'key' words level. While it is a familiar notion that a relatively small number of carrier words are repeated over and over again, it is not so well appreciated just how thinly the rest of the language is spread. Some surprisingly simple words may be encountered as seldom as one in a million times. This suggests a more hopeful explanation of the learning plateau. The low incidence of many words and the size of a working vocabulary, to be measured in thousands of words, emphasize the need for a period of absorption. The benefits take a long while to show through. The teaching task is to maintain morale and interest until they do, a task made infinitely easier by stimulating and appropriate material.

Materials and methods

The type and standard of materials for use by adult illiterates are steadily improving. The books produced by the B.B.C. *On the Move* and *Your Move* are outstanding. They are even better than many materials used for slow learners in secondary schools – where I hope they will now also be put into use.

Paradoxically, slow readers in secondary schools are more likely to be resentful of what they regard as childish reading books. Most regular attenders at adult literacy classes are keen enough to tolerate material designed for children. Some fairy stories and humorous books, such as those of Dr Seuss, appealed more to my students than specially written books which tended to suffer from self-conscious 'realism'. As one student put it, 'I have enough real life all day. I would rather read a fairy story.' If this observation is generally applicable, it is reassuring. For the economics of providing special books for a rather volatile market of illiterates and semi-literates are off-putting. There remains a shortage of starting material for absolute beginners. Tutors have to rely on either the language experience approach or phonics if they wish to avoid using an infant reading scheme. The drawback with language experience is the reticence and shyness of most adult illiterates, who are unlikely to come up with sentences of their own to analyze. Tutors gratefully seize upon a hobby or interest to study. (This can lead to problems – some pious students of mine insisted on reading the Bible right away.)

Although at first glance phonics is the most logical method for such beginners, and the one favoured by many volunteer tutors, it is in reality a stumbling block. The 'sight word' vocabulary of slow learning adults rose steadily while they were still finding it hard to 'synthesize' three letter words. These students became quite good readers and were still not able to manage phonics. If I had insisted on phonic proficiency at every stage the students would have been completely demoralized.

The lessons for teachers

Teachers who find time to take part in adult literacy classes will themselves learn a great deal. They will certainly find out more about the process of learning to read than emerges in teaching young children. They will be able to study what eventually becomes of their less successful pupils and perhaps redouble their efforts on that account. There is a pressing need for some kind of assessment of the performance of school leavers and the provision of further help for them, including advice on self-help.

It ought to be more widely realized that 'functional literacy', as it is called, which allows an individual to accommodate to a literate society, able to cope with signs, captions, forms, labels, instructions, notices, newspapers and so on, demands a reading standard *well beyond that attained by most primary children.* A 1973 study led by Donald Moyle (*Readability of Newspapers*) indicated that a reading age of at least thirteen is necessary to read a popular newspaper and make sense of simple forms and pamphlets. Politicians and secondary school teachers are wrong in blaming primary schools for reading failure. It is their problem as well. We have to get away from the notion of reading as merely a primary school 'subject', to be completed not later than the age of eleven – and devil take the hindmost. Of course the pressures on an individual teacher can be appreciated: the primary teacher wants to bring as many children as possible to a minimum standard of achievement; the secondary teacher feels he cannot take time from his subject in order to deal with what he sees as the rudiments. Perhaps, then, teachers should look to parents as allies in guiding children towards an ideal of mature, fluent and knowledgeable reading. But good intentions are not enough. I have drawn up a practical programme, ten pointers that teachers and parents together could use towards the goal of fluent reading, which forms the basis of the next chapter.

13 The Encouragement of Reading

A ten-point programme

Few reading experts would reject the help and involvement of parents in teaching children to read. However, most expertise in the teaching of reading has tended to stress the mechanics such as phonics, and the 'skills' such as 'auditory discrimination', which are outside the parent's ken. Parental help is perceived as secondary and mainly atmospheric. Personally, I don't believe in simply inviting parents to cheer from the sidelines. I see the encouragement of reading not just as something with which to oil the reading works, but as central to success. I see parents as being capable of detracting from the teacher's work by discouraging their children from reading – often inadvertently. Therefore the following advice is aimed equally at parents and teachers.

1) *Always trying to see things from child's point of view*

Most grown-ups assume reading is automatically a good thing and do not bother to persuade children of its benefits. But why should a small child want to read a book? He does it chiefly in order to imitate adults, as this is one of his chief motivations. It may not be strong enough to keep him going when reading turns out not to be as easy and pleasurable as it seemed.

Grown-ups may overlook the fact that often the only attractions of a book for a non-reader are the cover and illustrations. Make sure that children get plenty of good picture books, and don't expect them to respond even to well-written books without illustrations. In my opinion illustrations are dropped from books at far too early an age level, and children who are accustomed to the guidance and flavouring of pictures are suddenly out of touch. Adults, who are not exactly experimental in their own choice of reading, expect children to choose books with little more to go on than a title. In fact children go by favourites, often very old favourites indeed.

There are only two ways books can be introduced to children. One is by the illustrations and general presentation, the other is by adults recommending or reading them to children. Somehow adults must get away from merely propagating their own childhood favourites which, from the evidence of a Schools Council research study *Children and their Books* appear to have been *their* parent's favourites as well. Titles such as *Black Beauty, Treasure Island,* and *Little Women* head the list for junior children. Worthy as these books are, their popularity does seem to depend on their availability in schools. For example, *Black Beauty,* which topped the list, was available in all but a handful of primary schools in the study. *Finn Family Moomintroll* was in fiftieth place, presumably by virtue of the fact that it was available in only a quarter of the schools.

It is up to teachers and parents to observe and cater for children's own tastes and to broaden their own knowledge of what is available beyond 'the classics' and prize-winning books which may be too demanding for less able readers.

2) *Make positive use of television*

Nowadays it seems that adult tastes in books are more and more determined by T.V. programmes. A glance at any list of bestsellers, especially of paperbacks, is sure to reveal books that have been dramatized on T.V., books by T.V. personalities and books inspired by the cinema. T.V. has even greater magic for children. Any book derived from a children's T.V. programme is automatically appealing. Teachers and parents should make use of this, and also of the fact that children's interest in a subject that may be roused by T.V. programmes can be developed by means of books which would otherwise have no intrinsic appeal. Teachers are still too ready to deplore the influence of T.V. but, unless they realize its potency, they will overlook one of the most important influences on children's reading habits.

3) Children's television viewing should be rationed

It has been calculated that some children spend more time watching television than they do in class. The Schools Council survey showed that between a quarter and a third of ten-year-olds in working-class homes were putting in more than four hours viewing a night. The school day is altogether not much more than five hours long. This survey also showed that it was the younger age groups and those of least ability that viewed the most. Such indiscriminate viewing is bad for several reasons. It may mean that the parents have no interest in developing their children's taste or, indeed, in shaping their behaviour at all. Children get easily hooked on the kind of T.V. serials that set their adrenalin flowing, keeping them awake beyond their proper bedtime. Children over-stimulated by T.V. who stay up too late will feel tired the next day, and will be most likely to doze off or lose concentration in class during the quiet periods of reading and writing. My own recommendation is for a child to be allowed a maximum of one hour's viewing a day, the choice of which he can negotiate, providing it is within reasonable hours.

4) A proper share of time should be set aside for reading

This applies both at home and at school. Young children are usually so active and interested in such a variety of things that the day can go by without a chance of reading. Parents should always try to set aside a time in which they encourage their child to read for a short while, preferably while they stay and listen. Some teachers need similar advice. Quite busy and conscientious teachers may fill the curriculum with so many things that they skimp on independent reading time. Some formal schools rather frown on reading periods as a flippant use of time. Paradoxically, they may allow children who finish their work early to read a book as a treat: this virtually ensures that the children most in need of reading practice get least chance of it, as by and large they are the slowest to finish their formal work. There are different risks in informal classrooms. So much is going on and children have so many tasks there may be no leisure for reading. Certain children will avoid reading unless nudged into it by the teacher.

5) Books and reading must be made familiar and attractive

I have already suggested that from the children's point of view there may be little motivation to read, once the novelty has worn off, and difficulties arise in choosing interesting and enjoyable books. Without imposing adult tastes and values, teachers and parents should make sure children are familiar with the books they are going to read, by the simple device of reading them first to the children, with gusto. There should also be plenty of story-telling, story-reading and looking at picture books together. Parents have an advantage over teachers in being able to create a more intimate atmosphere when reading to a child. They can read more subtle material than a teacher, who is restricted by the most fidgety child in the group, could risk. A parent has more time to discuss pictures and to answer the questions the teacher has to curtail.

An indirect encouragement for beginning readers is to see their elders enjoying reading. The Schools Council survey mentions that 'even when social class and ability and attainment are held constant, there is a positive relationship between the amount of children's book reading and their parents' reading of library books'.

6) Make a place as well as a time for reading

Recently I was walking along the road with a mother who was telling me what a good reader her seven-year-old daughter was becoming. 'I hear her little voice piping over the telly,' she said. Sometimes even teachers do not appreciate the need to set aside a quiet corner for books, but it is just as much of a sin to have a sterile book corner or school library with beautiful decor, carpets, curtains and furnishings and not a child to be seen. What has gone wrong? It could be that the children are too busy doing tasks set by the teacher or that the books, while superficially attractive, reflect too much the teacher's taste and have no appeal for the children. The books may not have been properly introduced to the children. Children who have had to concentrate on written work for long periods may feel like doing something more active when they are given a free choice. The teachers may have imbued books and the book corner with a 'keep off the grass' quality. I know some teachers who insist on the children washing their hands before touching books.

The way to make a school book corner popular is for the teacher to spend some time herself sitting there reading, surrounded by the books she herself has made familiar to the children. Young children will soon show their customary curiosity and will gather round with their own books or simply stay with the teacher and hear her read.

218   *Reading Success*

7) *Show children how to get information from books*

Although there are countless information books for young children, they often remain unread in schools. The teacher does not read them to the children because they rarely hold an audience. (Occasionally an information book is as gripping as a good story. Titles such as *Whale's Way* and *Penguin's Way* by Joanna Johnston, are in this class.) The teacher does not read them aloud, so the children do not read them. Yet one of the most important skills a child can learn at school is how to find out, which entails using information and reference books. Too often where reading is seen as a once and for all attainment, children are not provided with the reading strategies that allow them to get the best out of information books. Too often, so-called topic work consists simply of copying chunks of text from information books. The best opportunity for teaching children how to find out is when children ask a good stumping question. The teacher or parent then says, 'I don't know the answer. Let's see if we can find out together.' Then follows a discussion of how best to go about it and a visit to the library to find the right information sources. Informal systems lend themselves far more easily to this type of learning then formal ones. For in the former there is usually a wider range of more accessible books. There is also more time to follow through a project, and a greater inclination to find out for oneself than to set store by the fixed answers in work books.

8) *Allow comics*

Many teachers view comics with disfavour, few parents think of them as educational, and yet, aside from the pure enjoyment children get out of comics, they are valuable reading practice. For some children they are the chief benefit of learning to read and for others the only private reading they get. Teachers and parents need not worry that comic reading displaces book reading. For the Schools Council survey found that among children aged ten to fourteen there was a 'tendency for heavy book reading to go hand in hand with heavy periodical reading' ('periodicals' referring mainly to comics). In any case teachers ought to be curious about the qualities that have kept such comics as *Dandy* and *Beano* as children's favourites from one generation to another. They could profitably study the comic strip convention that tells a story with a minimum of words because the pictures tell what is going on.

9) *Present books attractively*

We started by questioning the assumption that children would somehow find books attractive in themselves. I count myself among the people who find books en masse somewhat off putting. In a large library or bookshop, I suddenly feel there are too many books in the world. It gives me an inkling of how children must feel, faced with shelves of close packed titles and nothing to tempt the reader. For young children a boutique presentation of books is essential. They respond best to a few carefully chosen titles with their covers displayed. In school the display is best changed regularly by rotating the stock of books. Most young children conform to the sayings that variety is the spice of life and out of sight is out of mind. Parents should follow the ideal school practice and have a small selection of books at hand in the room where children spend most of their working hours, perhaps on the children's own bookshelf with drawing and writing materials nearby. It is no use expecting books to be read if they are kept in a cupboard or in a bedroom which is used only at night. It may also be a nice idea to put one or two children's books alongside the grown-up's current reading on a coffee table or side table.

10) Teach children how to use a library and a bookshop

Once again, it is a question of setting aside time for proper visits. Most children's libraries arrange special time each week for teachers to take their classes along. Parents are fortunate in having more time than the teacher to help children select books. (For all kinds of reasons, children are extremely conservative in their choice of books and if left entirely to their own devices some could well take out the same books over and over again.) Both libraries and bookshops are an under-used educational resource. In the next chapter I shall look at them alongside other resources available to encourage and improve reading.

14 Reading Resources

How to find good books

The word 'resource' has become fashionable in education and has gained a technical flavour. An article in a teacher's magazine described how a school turned its playground into a 'resource area'. The person who helps schools with printing leaflets, making slides and tapes, etc. is called a 'media resources officer'. Looking into the way this useful word has become part of education jargon I was reminded of another meaning of 'resource', a means of passing the time. 'Reading is a great resource' is the example given by the Oxford dictionary. This made me feel happier about calling this chapter 'Reading Resources', for although I am at pains to press every device into the service of learning to read, both the means and the end come down to good books. So I am now going to describe how to find good books and how to encourage children to read them.

The past few years have seen a cornucopia of colourful childrens' books. But I fear that in many cases more has gone into the packaging than the content. There are a lot of attractive picture books which make poor reading. The problem has been not of availability but of choosing well. Now that inflation is catching up with publishers and book buyers, the number of books produced is bound to go down and the purchasing power of schools and the public to be considerably reduced. How best do we ensure value for money?

221

Exhibitions and listings

Ideally, we should read all books before buying them for children. As this is physically impossible, it is necessary to seek some preliminary help and advice. The essential thing is to apply experience of tried and tested books to the choosing of new books. Children's books should never be purchased straight from a publisher's catalogue, however attractive they seem. Fortunately there are places where books have been gathered together and can be examined thoroughly. For example, the Centre for the Teaching of Reading, in Reading, has a permanent exhibition of books and other materials to help in the teaching of reading, such as audiovisual aids, programmed kits, reading games and so on. The Centre, apart from maintaining a comprehensive exhibition, issues excellent publications. *Learning to Read* by Betty Root catalogues most of the books available for the beginning reader and gives details of content, price and publisher. *Reading Skill Acquisition* by Bridie Raban provides a similar listing of non-book material such as reading games, workbooks, tapes, etc. *Retarded and Reluctant Readers* by Bridie Raban and Wendy Body is typical of the 'special lists' which cover such particulars as reading books for slower juniors. Among the reference books and guides intended mainly for teachers, there is one for parents, *Helping Your Child to Read,* by Ruth Nichols. An indispensable booklet in my opinion is *Individualized Reading* by Cliff Moon. A great deal of spade-work has gone into this compilation of books arranged according to their readability, and suggestions for a colour coding system whereby teachers can organize a wide variety of books into bands of graded difficulty. Every teacher should make an effort to visit the Centre for the Teaching of Reading.

The National Book League also has an exhibition of children's books with the emphasis on newly-published fiction and information books. My impression is that it is sadly under-used. It may be that too few people know about it, or that teachers are reluctant to spend their time merely in browsing through 'non-educational books'. For many teachers the expense of travelling to London may be a deterrent. However, the National Book League also organizes touring exhibitions of various selections of books, and produces helpful publications such as *Basic Reading Schemes, Books for the Multiracial Classroom, Information Books for the Slow Reader* and many other lists of books with succinct and expert critiques. Parents will be especially interested in the *Reading for Enjoyment* books lists prepared by Elaine Moss, who selects for the annual 'Children's Books of the Year' exhibition organized by the National Book League. The books in these lists can be hired as an exhibition.

Every year there is a splendid exhibition of school books organized by the London Head Teachers' Association. Similar exhibitions are organized by teachers in other parts of the country, notably at Caerleon, and Winchester and in the counties of Surrey and Durham. There are also frequent small private exhibitions held in hotel rooms and organized by seven or eight publishers getting together. The University of London Institute of Education has on permanent display all the school textbooks produced in this country which are currently available from the publishers for purchase. Looking at the country as a whole, however, I have a feeling that facilities are quite patchy. Some teachers in the north of England told me they were overwhelmed by the opportunity they had just enjoyed, at a publishers' exhibition, of examining the books they were thinking of buying. It would be a good idea for publishers to direct more time and money into travelling exhibitions bringing books and materials to teachers and parents; all three groups would benefit from comparing notes.

The local library: an under-used asset

Of course, no teacher or parent is very far from a permanent exhibition of children's books which has the added
advantage of built-in popularity – the local children's
library. As well as providing a friendly service for children,
most junior libraries now encourage borrowing by parents,
teachers and school classes.

Many local authorities run a school library service based
on the public libraries' stock. The usual arrangement is for
schools to borrow, say, a hundred books for a year, though
facilities vary between authorities. The secondary attrac-
tion of libraries is the ranging of activities they offer for
children during the early evening and in the school
holidays, such as clubs, talks, story sessions, games and
competitions. It is well worth parents encouraging their
children to use the local library and to go along with them
to help choose books and to find out about children's
interests and tastes.

Unfortunately, libraries are an under-used asset. Two-
thirds of ten-year-olds do not visit their local library and the
figure for non-use rises to three-quarters at the age of
fourteen – i.e., when children transfer to the senior library.
All of this suggests that schools are failing to interest their
children in reading and that a majority of parents are out of
touch. It could well be that out of school a lot of children
are heartily sick of books, which they associate with boring
lessons. I wonder if the key does not lie in the unfailing
popularity of good picture books, with older children as
well as with infants. I wish libraries and schools were less
priggish about those admirable adventure stories in comic
strip form, the 'Tin-Tin' and 'Asterix' books. They help to
bridge the gap between picture-assisted reading and the
real thing. Their 'what-happens-next' feeling spurs the
young reader on, and they stand up to any amount of rereading.

Favourites

It is no use going to the library and expecting to see at once children's favourite books. By definition the most popular books are scarcely on the shelves. It pays to quiz the librarian on children's likes, especially as measured by the reserve lists. When I did this recently, I found the top favourites included *Charlie and the Chocolate Factory* and other books by Roald Dahl; *The Little Ghost, The Little Witch* and *Robber Hotzenplotz* by Otfried Preussler; Alf Proysen's 'Mrs Pepperpot' stories and Michael Bond's 'Paddington Bear' series, plus the 'Asterix' and 'Tin-Tin' books mentioned above. The name of Enid Blyton is never missing from the reserve list. Close behind in popularity come Willard Price's adventure stories, *Charlotte's Web* by E.B. White, the 'Bobby Brewster' stories by H.E. Todd, and the 'Narnia' stories by C.S. Lewis.

The younger users of the library rate most highly the Collins' 'Beginner Books' edited by Dr Seuss, the 'Topsy and Tim' series by Jean and Gareth Adamson; Angela Banner's 'Ant and Bee' books and the Reverend W. Awdrey's 'Little Engine' series. Across all age groups, fairy tales remain as popular as modern stories I have mentioned, especially when expertly retold by Ruth Manning Sanders, Andrew Lang, Mollie Clark or Vera Southgate. Children show their determination to exert their taste in their treatment of poetry shelves. Between many untouched volumes they ferret out the nonsense rhymes. Edward Lear is a firm favourite, other winners are *Oh What Nonsense, Rhyme Giggles and Joke Giggles, Beastly Boys and Ghastly Girls*, all poems collected by William Cole and illustrated by Tomi Ungerer. Older children prefer a touch of mystery: *The Iron Man* by Ted Hughes has become a modern classic. Ghost stories score highly with the over tens. Perennial favourites include *Black Beauty, Pippi Longstocking* and *The Silver Sword*. Among schoolboy heroes 'Jennings', has the lead over 'William Brown' and 'Billy Bunter'. The titles and series listed above reveal the main ingredients of children's choice; a successful series or character; a well-established author; occasionally a particular theme often leading to a request to the librarian for 'more of the same'. All these factors demonstrate children's conservatism. Apart from television the major influence for innovation and experiment is the school, but the schools themselves tend to be conservative in the choice of titles they keep. More children's books are listed in Chapter 3 under *A shopping list of books* and in the bibliography at the end of this book.

A really live bookshop

There is a distressing lack of children's book shops, reflecting our somewhat philistine tendencies as a nation (indicated by the 'Books Upstairs' sign I saw in a large branch of a chain once devoted to book retailing). For grown-ups the lack of good bookshops may be offset to a certain extent by the availability of paperbacks at newsagents and general stores, but good children's bookshops or departments of a main book store are few and far between. Many parents and teachers might not realize what they are missing unless they visit an outstanding children's bookshop, such as the famous Children's Book Centre at 229 Kensington Church Street, London W8, which encourages visits by school parties 'to see a really live bookshop in action'. This bookshop has become so successful that it is now the largest children's bookshop in the world and runs several services, such as boxed exhibitions of books for parents' evenings or school events, newsletters promoting Puffin books, the supplying of school bookshops under licence, competitions, and the organizing of special events such as story-readings and craft demonstrations.

Theoretically our population of ten million schoolchildren could support several equivalents of the Children's Book Centre. Is it then teachers' or parents' fault for not valuing reading books highly enough? Parents are to be criticized if they don't buy books at all, or if they go by the often inadequate choice of children's books at the local newsagent's (especially a volume from the most commonly used reading scheme). Yet the fact that these books are stocked so widely shows that parents want to help their children but lack guidance. Teachers are to be faulted if they do not provide such guidance, if they make early reading a dutiful chore, and if they do not try to make up for the lack of a local bookshop. There are two ways in which schools themselves can sell children's books to parents. One is to set up a school bookshop, the other is to start a book club.

School bookshops

School bookshops 'can range from plush emporia that can challenge many a city bookshop in their range of titles, to creative corners of primary schools where parents and children mingle among the wire racks and chipboard displays.' The quote is from a *Times Educational Supplement* article singing the praises of Peter Kennerly, who for the best part of two decades has worked to establish the concept and the reality of the school bookshop while continuing his job as a teacher and college lecturer. He has now written a book called *The School Bookshop*. As a result of the efforts of Peter Kennerly and the people he inspired, there are now seven thousand school bookshops and a great deal of know-how, all of which can be learned by contacting the School Bookshop Association. This organization is in fact an offshoot of the National Book League which, as I write, is contemplating leaving its address at 7 Albemarle Street, London W1.

Free hard work

I hesitate to criticize such a splendid idea as school bookshops, but there is a considerable disadvantage. The school usually takes its stock from a local bookshop, or nationally from the Children's Book Centre, or Books for Students Ltd (addresses in appendix), on a sale or return basis. I wonder if the supplier does not get by far the better of the deal in the shape of the free hard work of teachers and parents. However dedicated the helpers involved, their time is not limitless. It has been estimated that running a school-bookshop can take anything from two to five hours a week. This is a great deal to ask of a teacher. The risk of a bookshop closing down because the moving spirit gets tired or leaves the school is great. The key to a successful bookshop is the availability of parental volunteers to help with the work of storing, ordering and collecting stock, manning the shop, handling cash, recording the sales, doing the accounts, and keeping up the publicity and propaganda when the novelty wears off. (The Publishers' Association licence is needed too.) In some areas there is always a supply of parents willing and able to take on such tasks. Elsewhere mothers may be at work all day and, because of the lack of volunteers, may favour the alternative of a book club, which is much easier to run.

Book clubs

Most of the work for a book club is done by the suppliers, as with the adult versions which are advertised in newspapers and magazines. A wide selection of club choices is offered together with order forms. Parents and children decide what they want and send back the completed order form and the money. What the school gets out of it is either a cash discount or free books. The drawback, of course, is that however satisfactory the choice, it must always be limited. The Puffin Club has only Puffin books, the Ladybird Club has only Ladybirds. One of the biggest book clubs, Scholastic, promotes a lot of American material, which tends to be hit-or-miss. The Children's Book Club sends copies of each book on its list, so that the children can examine them before making a choice. The specimen copies may be sold or returned.

Awareness of good books

I favour book clubs because, while maintaining enthusiasm for book buying by means of regular offers, they do not allow children to take them for granted, or the parents to feel unreasonable cash demands are being made on them. However, in my experience of school bookshops and book clubs, I have noticed that children tend always to choose the familiar. So a conservative choice, within the book clubs' already 'play safe' choice, stifles experimentation. But there is no doubt that book clubs develop awareness of good books in homes where the parents would not buy them otherwise. Bargain price book clubs for children have started to be advertised in the national press on similar lines to adult book clubs, where a number of introductory books can be had for a song, provided there is a commitment to regular choices. I have been impressed with the careful pre-selection and the good value they offer. One such club is the Skylark Children's Book Club for seven-to ten-year-olds. After an initial low price introductory offer, there is a monthly choice of a quality hardback book and a free monthly magazine containing short stories, puzzles and things to do and make. It is a pity that Skylark do not also offer alternative, cheaper, paperback titles. Parents who are at a loss as to what books to buy for their children, might find such a book club, with titles chosen by a panel of editors and teachers, a great boon. I only hope that book

clubs do not make parents lazy about going to bookshops
and libraries and encouraging children's individual tastes
in books.

Teachers are well served by reviews of children's books,
both text books and general books, in their specialist press.
The Times Educational Supplement, Child Education, and
Junior Education have comprehensive and helpful book
reviews, although they provide less information about
non-book materials such as cassette tapes. The general
public enjoys less good advice since the national press,
radio and television give only sporadic coverage, with the
chief emphasis on fiction and literary values. There are a
number of publications which both parents and teachers
would find useful in choosing children's books. Such
specialist periodicals include *Books for Your Children*
edited by Anne Wood and Jean Russell, which is brought
out four times a year for a subscription of £2.00 per
annum; and *Growing Point* edited by Margery Fisher, with
nine issues a year for a subscription of £2.00 per annum.
Useful book lists are also issued by the Federation of
Children's Book Groups (all addresses listed at the end of
this book).

Although, with a certain amount of effort, information
and reviews can be obtained, they are no substitute for
actually trying out books on children. Naturally, teachers
are in a better position to do this than parents. Most
teachers have a good knowledge of what children like and
ought to like – but parents may be surprised how seldom
children's choice of titles reflects the prize-winning type of
children's books. Although I am not against literary prizes
for children's authors who are often under-regarded and
under-rewarded, I feel that too seldom are the children
consulted. Only occasionally and in a gimmicky way, for
example at Christmas, will a newspaper ask children for
their views on various books. Although we live in a
consumer society, children tend to be overlooked as the

customers for reading books. I should like to see medals awarded to books by panels of young readers.

School and classroom libraries

Obviously a most important reading resource is a well-planned, well-stocked and well-used school library. Unfortunately such a facility is rarer than one might think. Only very new schools, or old schools with rooms to spare for conversion, have had actual libraries built in to them. The classroom 'library' or 'book corner' is more common, especially in infant schools. At their best they can be just as attractive as a separate room, when made comfortable with chairs and tables, cushions and carpets, and books appealingly displayed. Yet even in a small classroom, the 'library' may be under-used if it is not an inviting place.

A separately housed school library creates difficulties of use and supervision. Without active encouragement it may not occur to children to visit the library, but teachers may hesitate to allow them to go to browse without an adult present. Ideally, a library needs to be supervised by a teacher working there with groups of children, or by an ancillary helper who will see that the books are put away correctly and the library left tidy. Usually the job of organizing, stocking and maintaining the school library is taken up by a teacher as a 'post of responsibility', extra to her normal work.

Looking after even a small library is a demanding task. The books have to be chosen and bought, a suitable system of classification has to be devised, and the room has to be maintained. In a primary school library simplicity is the key. The books could be arranged by a simple colour coding. For example, a series of coloured spots on reading books to indicate the level of difficulty and a similar system based on coloured shapes to classify topic books. If the Dewey system is used, it needs simplifying for primary

children. There is no need for an elaborate record of
borrowings. The hard work goes into the grading and
marking of the books. The skill goes into the choice of
books and evaluation of new titles, which are jobs that all
members of staff should take part in, thereby making sure
that every teacher is familiar with the children's books and
their preferences. The school library is the logical place for
audiovisual aids such as tape recorders and loop projectors.
Teachers can record stories on tape and children can then
follow the text. There are also plenty of commercially
recorded stories. The B.B.C. produced an excellent series
to accompany its 'Listening and Reading' programmes,
which can now be purchased from Penguin Educational.
This outstanding series includes adaptations of *The Iron
Man* by Ted Hughes, *A Lion at School* by Philippa Pearce,
and the traditional tale *The Wolf and the Seven Little Kids*,
which are my favourites.

I also recommend the tapes and records produced by
Scholastic publications to accompany some of their titles.
Weston Wood Studios produce film strips of various well-
known picture books. Children greatly enjoy these audio-
visual devices. But potentially the most exciting way of
introducing books and reading is through television.

How television got it right in the end

The power of demonstration that television has, and its
hold over children, can be put to powerful educative use.
In the case of reading, this has happened only after a great
deal of trial and error. People seem to have wrongly
assumed that you could pack all that was necessary about
the teaching of reading into a short programme of fifteen
minutes. The further mistake was made of using television
simply as an electronic classroom and overlooking the
variety of techniques at the disposal of the television
educator. Flash cards can be just as boring when shown by

a lady on the television screen as by a lady in the classroom. Like everything else connected with the teaching of reading, television reading lessons demand a lot of preparation on the part of both the producers and the presenter. The most effective television programmes about reading will be based on programme notes, which the teacher must study well ahead. She must look to the programme itself to stimulate interest and motivate children to follow up the aspects of reading that the programme has touched on. Ideally the teacher should have previewed the programme and have got the follow-up material ready. Without this before-and-after activity, television reading is a waste of time.

Among much forgettable material there are two outstanding series which are models of the right approach. I hope they will be repeated or turned into films or video tapes. The first is *Reading with Lenny,* which features ventriloquist Terry Hall with his famous puppet Lenny the Lion. The usual format is for Terry to read Lenny a story from his own reading series, 'Kevin the Kitten' readers. Lenny then goes on to try to read the story captions himself, running his paw along the line of text as he does so. Lenny gets very excited and pleased with himself when he discovers that he can read. This excitement rubs off on the children, who are delighted to have a go themselves at the 'Kevin the Kitten' books. Lenny provides motivation in three ways: by introducing the reading books and showing they are good books to read; by Lenny's infectious enjoyment of reading; and by allowing children to identify with Lenny, a beginner like them. *Reading with Lenny* would be an ideal programme for parents to watch with their pre-school children.

The other recommended T.V. series on reading is a B.B.C. programme called *Words and Pictures,* which also uses puppetry to introduce reading books by dramatizing them. Usually the choice is of a good picture story book with a simple repetitive plot. *Chicken Licken* is the classic example. The puppet play is accompanied by captions and speech bubbles for the audience to read. After each story there is an entertaining phonic exercise, good enough to create interest in the phonic worksheets which are part of the follow-up work. Yet I feel that the chief value of this series, as with Lenny, is that the books are introduced in such an exuberant way that the children cannot wait to read the stories themselves. This is far more valuable than any actual reading tuition that appears on the screen.

Radio is intrinsically less suitable for teaching reading, since reading is largely a visual skill. However B.B.C. Radio has contributed to the teaching of reading in other ways, for example, by means of story-telling and talk programmes about the subject. One such programme was a series called 'Teaching Young Readers', in which teachers described and discussed their methods and techniques. However, the most useful thing that came out of this series was a handbook entitled *Teaching Young Readers* published by B.B.C. Publications. It is a down-to-earth basic manual, outlining the organization and materials needed for teaching reading. It is also a very good reference book for reading sources and resources.

How publishers still haven't quite got it right

Finally, there is a reading resource which can get overlooked – the publishers, who tempt us with thousands of books a year. Although I suggested it was wrong simply to choose children's books from a catalogue alone, it is well worth studying catalogues to see what is available, to keep up to date with prices and other information, and, of course, to order books. As one of our chief educational resources, publishers are not always as easy to deal with as they ought to be. Some time ago all the publishers in the Western world decided to entrust their ordering systems to computers, and every book now has a so-called 'Standard Book Number' which runs to ten digits. For a start, this is not always easy to recognize as some publishers break up the 'SBN' into two different parts, putting, for example, the prefix in the introduction to the catalogue and the suffix in a list at the end. The otherwise welcome trend towards breaking down thick volumes into many slim, easily finished reading books, leads to a proliferation of numbers. It turns the ordering of books from a pleasure into a chore. Some good books do not even get ordered because the codes are too obscure or impossible to find. I entreat all publishers of reading books to put all relevant information, such as the complete SBN and the price, beside each catalogue entry and to provide separate numbers to cover the ordering of a set of books. I suspect that some publishers still put their own convenience before that of the customer or even before the encouragement of sales. However, most publishers do offer schools an inspection copy service which is always worth using.

15 Reading Success

Attitudes

One difficulty in writing a book about learning to read is keeping up to date with the shifts of public opinion. No sooner had I got used to being assailed by friends, acquaintances and parents about the 'drop in reading standards' than along came Her Majesty's Inspectors with a report on 'Primary Education in England' (1978) that proved standards had been rising all the time. We shall never avoid these apparent lurches of performance and policy until we stop worrying about 'the reading problem'. We need to study the causes of reading success as thoroughly as we have looked at reading failure. When we have better measures of success and failure, the problem will be revealed as an opportunity. I have earlier argued the case for a more sensitive, realistic and purposeful set of reading tests. These alone would point the way to a more positive and expansive role for the teaching of reading. My impression is that a lot of early reading teaching is on the right lines and I am convinced we can look forward to steady progress, i.e., reading standards continuing to rise. But if we want to move faster, we must change our attitudes.

We must get rid of the awe of reading

Awe of reading makes it a matter of techniques to be understood only by experts. It may be that such residual awe, and academic attempts to preserve reading as a mystery, are deep rooted in the public mind. As late as the seventeenth century the following passage was literally a vital reading text: 'Have mercy upon me, O God, according to thy loving kindness; according unto the multitude of thy tender mercies blot out my transgressions.' A prisoner who could read this verse was able to claim 'benefit of clergy', in other words, he need not be tried before a secular court and so saved his neck. Benefit of clergy was completely abolished only in 1827.

We must absorb the lessons of psycholinguistics

Psycholinguistics is so far the most convincing explanation of what really happens between eye and mind in reading and learning to read. Universal literacy was a product of nineteenth-century progress. We are still dealing with the aftermath and, perhaps not surprisingly, a lot of reading teaching still has a Victorian air – pious and mechanical. To teach an entire nation its letters was a superhuman task and perhaps could only have been achieved by 'industrial' methods. (The high water mark of this thinking is surely the giant comprehensive school offering 'economies of scale'.) Now, at the primary level, we have become more relaxed and individualistic. We are better positioned to reflect the idea that reading and writing are just as much products of the human mind as of the classroom. Reading ought, upon a technical examination, to be extraordinarily difficult, verging upon the impossible. Instead, in practice, reading is rather difficult to start with and tends to get easier – unless it is artificially constricted in some way. The key to it all is the way our mental computer, responding to the complex programme built into language, becomes near perfect at predicting 'what comes next'. In a few individuals the predictability of language allows them to memorize their reading with ease. There was an eighteenth-century actor called Macklin who had such an ability, and the writer Samuel Foote determined to catch him out. Macklin went off in a huff when faced with this reading test that Foote devised for him:

> So she went into the garden to cut a cabbage-leaf to make an apple pie, and at the same time a great she-bear came running up the street and popped its head into the shop. 'What! no soap?' So he died, and she very imprudently married the barber. And there were present the Picninnies, Jobillies, and Garyulies, and the Grand Panjandrum himself, with the little red button a top, and they all fell to playing the game of catch as catch can till the gunpowder ran out at the heels of their boots.

We must learn to treat children themselves as the finest 'reading resource'

Whenever a crisis is reported in the teaching of reading, educationists are likely to wring their hands and call for more teachers, more non-teaching helpers, smaller classes, better schools, more books and equipment, and so on. These demands for extra resources are perfectly justified. They would undoubtedly lead to more efficient reading teaching. But they all take more time and money than we have to spare.

We could, however, increase reading achievements immediately if more teachers could be persuaded to change their attitude and accept humbly that the chief role of a reading teacher is to help children teach themselves to read. For some teachers this takes a lot of swallowing. Perhaps it is the way they teach – vocabulary drills, short unrevealing reading sessions, obligatory correction of mistakes – that never allows them to discover the extent of children's contributions, in the way of language, logic, intuition and experimental 'mistakes', to the business of learning to read. Perhaps it goes deeper than that, down to an assumption that to be taught properly a child must be treated as a *tabula rasa*, a clean slate on which only the teacher can form the proper characters.

At this point in the book, having earlier quoted two unusual reading tests, I hoped finally to describe with suitable extracts how a famous fictional character taught himself to read. Unfortunately, for copyright reasons, I am unable to quote the eloquent and plausible account of how the young Tarzan of the Apes wrestled with, and eventually mastered, reading. I can only direct readers to the original book by Edgar Rice Burroughs.

However, truth is not to be outdone by fiction. A real-life example exists of a child who learned to read without any sort of teacher. The case was studied in 1969 by an American researcher, Dr Jane Torrey. She came across a five-year-old negro pre-school boy whose ability to read was thought by his mother to be a gift from God. Apparently he had taught himself to read by means of television commercials. (Dr Torrey established that on American television some forty words an hour are simultaneously shown and pronounced.) His first reading primers were the labels on the cans in the kitchen.

The existence of child prodigies is, of course, not a reason for doing without teachers, and leaving children to their own devices. But it does remind us of the great capacity for learning that children possess. The point, though, is that this little negro boy, while a reading prodigy, was in no way an intellectual prodigy. Nor could he be regarded as socially privileged. He was quite ordinary in other activities, although intensely competitive in his reading. I think, therefore, it would be worthwhile quoting Jane Torrey's conclusions from her study. Her first hypothesis is that 'reading is learned, not taught', and after discussing the 'key questions' 'How does something I can say look in print?' and 'What does that print say?', she concludes that however useful high verbal ability and high cultural privilege may be in stimulating reading, neither is necessary'.

We must encourage teachers to adopt a confident, professional attitude

I hope I have shown in this book that reading success comes essentially from helping children to learn, and emphatically not from teaching reading *at* children. Yet some teachers may well be dismayed by my advice to spend more time in the seemingly passive and 'unprofessional' task of hearing children read. But the observation, support, preparation and assessment necessary for the effective teaching of reading call for the highest skill and dedication. They can be easily overlooked. In an informal classroom it is tempting to allow reading to be displaced by more exciting and glamorous activities. At the opposite pole, a formal teacher can find, with an easy conscience, that reading makes no great professional demands – the onus is on the pupils. In both cases the devil takes not only the hindmost but the foremost. The Inspectors' report, that I mentioned above, criticized schools for not stimulating and 'stretching' the more able readers.

I believe it would be extremely dangerous for anyone to try to impose 'good practice'. The freedom British schools enjoy is priceless. Uniformity, even in a good cause, is not worth a light. I have my own views of what constitutes 'bad practice'. I think it is the result of defensive attitudes. Teachers who lack confidence or who are browbeaten, will take on protective coloration. If they are perceived as glorified child-minders, that is what they will be. If they are seen as social workers, they will be more interested in changing society than improving a child's reading. Others will take refuge in jargon and patent methods, or retreat into a perfect past.

As I see it, good practice will be properly enhanced and

exemplified by means of high status and professional standards for teachers to live up to. I am not sure, however, that I would go along the route taken by a group of American primary teachers. The Maryland State Teachers Association, reports the *Washington Post,* is running an advertising campaign to improve the status of the teacher. The television commercials will show busy kindergartens, marching bands with plumed hats and 'one white-haired, bespectacled woman by a blackboard who looks like everyone's idea of a primary school teacher'. Billboards and bumper stickers will carry the slogan, 'If you can read this, Thank Your Teacher'. Mmmmm.

Appendix

Books and pamphlets mentioned in the text

* denotes recommended reading

*Arvidson, Dr G.L., **Learning to Spell,** Wheaton, 1970.
Baldwin, Gertrude, **Patterns of Sound,** Chartwell Press, 1967.
*B.B.C. Publications, **On the Move,** 1975.
*B.B.C. Publications, **Your Move,** 1976.
*Bowie, Janetta, **Penny Buff: Clydeside School in the Thirties,** Constable, 1975.
*Bullock Report, **A Language for Life,** H.M.S.O., 1975.
*Dean, Joan, **Teaching Young Readers,** B.B.C. Publications, 1976.
Diack and Daniels, **The Standard Reading Tests,** Chatto Educ., 1958.
Doman, Glenn, **Teach Your Baby to Read,** Jonathan Cape, 1965.
*Edwards, R.P.A., and Gibbon, V., **Words Your Children Use,** Burke, 1973.
Gattegno, Caleb, **Reading with Words in Colour,** Educational Explorers, 1969.
Goodacre, Elizabeth, **Children and Learning to Read,** Routledge and Kegan Paul, 1971.
*Hughes, Felicity, **Reading and Writing Before School,** Jonathan Cape, 1971.
Hughes, John M., **Reading and Reading Failures,** Evans, 1975.
Kennerly, Peter, **The School Bookshop,** Ward Lock Educ., 1976.
*Moon, Cliff, **Individualized Reading,** Univ. of Reading Centre for Teaching of Reading, 1975.
*Moon, Cliff, and Raban, Bridie, **Penguins in Schools,** Penguin, 1977.
Morris, Joyce, **Reading in the Primary School,** N.F.E.R., 1959.
Moyle, Donald, *et al,* **Readability of Newspapers,** Edge Hill College of Educ., 1971.

National Book League, **Basic Reading Schemes: Booklist** (Anne Leyton Pearce), 1975.

National Book League, **Books for the Multiracial Classroom** (Judith Elkin), 1976.

National Book League, **Information Books for the Slow Reader** (Donald Wilkinson), 1970.

National Book League, **Reading for Enjoyment with 2-5 year-olds** (Elaine Moss), 1975.

Nichols, Ruth, **Helping Your Child to Read,** Univ. of Reading Centre for Teaching of Reading, 1974.

*Peters, Margaret, **Spelling Caught or Taught,** Routledge and Kegan Paul, 1974.

*Peters, Margaret, **Success in Spelling,** Cambridge Inst. of Educ., 1970.

*Plowden Report, **Children and their Primary Schools,** H.M.S.O., 1967.

Raban, Bridie, **Reading Skill Acquisition,** Univ. of Reading Centre for Teaching of Reading, 1974.

Raban, Bridie, and Body, Wendy, **Retarded and Reluctant Readers,** Univ. of Reading Centre for Teaching of Reading, 1975.

Rice Burroughs, Edgar, **Tarzan of the Apes,** New English Library, 1975.

*Root, Betty, **Learning to Read,** Univ. of Reading Centre for Teaching of Reading, 1975.

*Schonell, F.J., **The Psychology and Teaching of Reading,** Oliver and Boyd, 1974.

*Schools Council, **Children and Their Books** (Whitehead *et al*), Macmillan Educ., 1977.

Schools Council, **i.t.a., an independent evaluation** (Warburton and Southgate), Murray and Chambers, 1969.

Schools Council, **Teaching English to West Indian Children,** Evans Methuen Educ., 1970.

*Smith, Frank, **Comprehension and Learning,** Holt, Rinehart and Winston, 1975.

*Smith, Frank, **Psycholinguistics and Reading,** Holt, Rinehart and Winston, 1973.

*Smith, Frank, **Reading,** Cambridge Univ. Press, 1978.

*Smith, Frank, **Understanding Reading: a psycholinguistic analysis of reading and learning to read,** Holt, Rinehart and Winston, 1971.

*Spencer, Herbert, **The Visible Word,** Lund Humphries, 1968

Children's books recommended in the text

Ardizzone, Edward, **Little Tim and the Brave Sea Captain,** Oxford University Press, 1955.

Clarke, Mollie, **The Remarkable Rat,** Mayflower, 1972.

Edwards, Dorothy, **My Naughty Little Sister** (Puffin), Penguin, 1970.

Hall, Terry, **Watch Me** (Laugh and Learn), George Philip Alexander, 1975.

Huchet Bishop, Claire, **The Five Chinese Brothers,** Bodley Head, 1961.

Johnstone, Joanna, **Penguin's Way,** World's Work Press, 1964.

Johnstone, Joanna, **Whale's Way,** World's Work Press, 1966.

Scott Foresman Reading System, **The Great Big Enormous Turnip,** Heinemann, 1968.

Seuss, Dr, **Beginner Books,** Collins (many titles).

Seuss, Dr, **The Sneetches,** Collins, 1965.

Thackray, Derek and Lucy, **This is My Colour,** George Philip Alexander, 1974.

Ungerer, Tomi, **The Three Robbers,** Methuen, 1964.

Other recommended children's books are listed in Chapter 3 under *A shopping list of books,* and in Chapter 14 under *Favourites.*

Some simple dictionaries

Beginner Book Dictionary, Dr Seuss, Collins, 1965.

Best Word Book Ever, Richard Scarry, Hamlyn, 1970.

Ladybird Picture Dictionary and Spelling Book, Ladybird, 1973.

My Book of Words, Hulme and Hulme, A. and C. Black, 1970.

Picture Dictionary, Lavinia Derwent, Burke, 1969.

Picture Dictionary, Richard Hefter, Picture Lions, 1970.

Picture Dictionary, Lavinia Derwent, Collins, 1978.

Picture Dictionary, J. Taylor and T. Ingleby, Longmans, 1969.

First Writing Dictionary, T.J. Hulme and T.F. Carnody, A. and C. Black, 1972.

Young Set Dictionary One, Two, Three and **Four,** Amy L. Brown, John Downing and John Sceats, Chambers, 1970, 1971, 1972, and 1973.

Appendix 245

Periodicals which review children's books

Growing Point Edited by Margery Fisher, Ashton Manor, Ashton, Northants.
Books For Your Children Edited by Anne Wood and Jean Russell, 90 Gillhurst Road, Harborne, Birmingham 17.
Book Window Edited by Margaret Walker, 1 Beaumont Gate, Glasgow G12.
Child Education Edited by Annie Smith, Evans Brothers Ltd, Montague House, Russell Square, London WC1.
Junior Education Edited by Annie Smith, Evans Brothers Ltd, Montague House, Russell Square, London WC1.
School Bookshop News Edited by Peter Kennerly, School Bookshop Association, 7 Albemarle Street, London W1.
The School Librarian Edited by Norman Furlong, School Library · Association, Victoria House, 29-31 George Street, Oxford.
The Times Educational Supplement New Printing House Square, Gray's Inn Road, London WC1.

Useful addresses

The National Book League, 7 Albemarle Street, London W1.

Centre for the Teaching of Reading, School of Education, University of Reading, Reading, Berks.

Educational Publishers Council, 19 Bedford Square, London WC1.

British Equipment Association, Sunley House, 10 Gunthorpe Street, London E1.

The Children's Book Centre, 229 Kensington Church Street, London W8.

The School Bookshop Association (off-shoot of the National Book League), 7 Albemarle Street, London W1.

Books for Students Ltd, Catteshall Lane, Godalming, Surrey.

The Puffin Book Club, Penguin Books, Harmondsworth, Middlesex.

Children's Book Club, 4 Bishops Place, Paignton, Devon.

Ladybird Book Club, 4 Bishops Place, Paignton, Devon.

Bookworm Club, Napier Place, Cumbernauld, Glasgow.

Skylark Book Club, P.O. Box 19, Swindon, Wilts.

Scholastic (See-Saw, Lucky, Chip and Scoop Clubs), 161 Fulham Road, London SW3.

Federation of Children's Book Groups (Secretary – Alan Counsel), 17 Andrew Close, Ailsworth, Peterborough.

Books for Your Children, Church Street, Haxey, Nr Doncaster, South Yorkshire.

Books for Children (a book club for parents to use), Gloucester House, Dyer Street, Cirencester, Glos.

Useful toys

The following toys will help to improve children's reading and writing. They can all be bought by parents from James Galt's toyshops.

> Plywood letters (script and capitals)
>
> Linking wooden letters
>
> Picture word lotto
>
> Picture letter dominoes

How What and Where ('a self corrective activity designed to ensure correct usage of thirty-six essential prepositions verbs and adjectives'). Wooden word maker (three letters which swivel to give different combinations).

My Picture Word Games

Scrabble for Juniors
Alphabet friezes by Bruna, Michael Spinks and Gallery Five.

INDEX

McNally, J.: Key *Words to Literacy*, 92
meaning: shades of, 32-4
mirror writing, 139-40
miscue analysis, 164-6
mistakes: allowing child to find, 138; criticizing, 139, 200
'Monster' books, 81-2
Moon, Cliff, 70-1; *Individualized Reading*, 71, 82, 106, 222; *Penguins in Schools*, 170-2
Morris, Joyce: *Reading in the Primary School*, 195
Moss, Elaine, 223
motivation, 20, 53-5, 199-200, 213-14
Moyle, Donald: *Readability of Newspapers*, 212
multiple choice tests, 151
Murray, W.: *Key Words to Literacy*, 92: Ladybird Reading Scheme: extract, 51
My Naughty Little Sister, 176-7

National Book League, 222-3, 227
National Survey Form 6 reading tests, 157
Neale Analysis of Reading Ability, 153, 155-6, 167
'news': children writing, 133-4
Nichols, Ruth: *Helping Your Child to Read*, 222
Nisbet, R. Munro, 50
non-book resources, 73-9
nonsense words, 142
Norway: school age, 194-5
nursery education, 191

O'Donnell, M., 50
'One, Two, Three and Away' series, 56
On the Move, 210
Orwell, George: *1984*, 176

paper: for writing, 136-7
parents: buying reading materials, 79-82; help by, 201-2; helping before school, 102; helping with reading, 122-3; helping with writing

and spelling, 145-7; introducing books to children, 172-3; looking at picture books with children, 102; providing motivation, 200; teaching babies, 100-2; ten-point programme for, 213-20
Patterns of Sound, 23
Peabody Language Development Kit, 186
Penguins in Schools, 170-2
personality: traits helpful to reading, 196-7; traits of West Indians, 192
Peters Margaret, 144; *Spelling Caught or Taught*, 141; *Success in Spelling*, 141
phonemes, 24
phonetics: rudiments of, 119-20
phonics, 22-9; for adult learners, 211; need for, 118; in reading tests, 157; rules, 17-18, 93; starting, 104; variations on, 38-44; variations on: annotation, 44; variations on: i.t.a., 38-43
picture books, 102, 214
picture dictionaries, 129
pictures: importance of, 58-64
Pitman, Sir James, 27, 38
playgroups, 191
Plowden Report, 202
poetry, 33
practice, daily: need for, 209
praise: need for, 200
pre-reading skills, 98-9
pre-school playgroups, 191
programme, ten-point, 213-20
progress; getting sense, of, 66-8; in fits and starts, 104-5; making, 104-23; measuring, 148-68
pseudo-science,. 76-9
psycholinguistics, 10, 13-15, 237
Psycholinguistics and Reading, 13
Psychology and Teaching of Reading, 34
publishers: dealing with, 234-5
Puffin Club, 229
punctuation, 140

Raban, Bridie: *Penguins in Schools*, 170-2: *Reading Skill Acquisition*, 73, 222; *Retarded and Reluctant Readers*, 222
radio, 234
Randall, Beverley, 120
readability, 70-1
Readability of Newspapers, 212
Reading, 13
reading: place for, 217; time spent on, 86-7, 89-90, 216
reading age: accuracy, 150; meaning, 150-1
Reading and Reading Failures, 11-12
Reading and Writing Before School, 101
Reading for Enjoyment, 223
Reading in the Primary School, 195
reading kits, 73, 76-9
reading laboratories, 76-9
reading materials, 48-82; introducing, 107-10; non-book resources, 73-9; for parents to buy, 79-82; teacher reading to class first, 20, 108-10, 216-17; unsuitable, 108-9
reading readiness, 97-9; tests for, 98
reading records, 168
reading resources, 221-35
reading schemes, 48-73; differences in vocabularies, 68-70; important elements, 49; individualized, 70-1; mixing, 67-8; readability, 70-1
reading sessions: time allotted to, 86-7, 89-90, 216
Reading Skill Acquisition, 73, 222
reading standards, 158
reading tests: age bias, 153-6; case for, 148-9; cultural bias, 159-60; dated, 157-9; diagnostic, 162-4, 167; effects of cultural changes on, 156-7; group tests, 151-2; inaccuracy of results, 157-8; individual tests, 152-3; miscue analysis, 164-6; multiple choice. 151; outdated words in, 158-9;